Shine On! 4

Helen Casey

Student Book

Practice

OXFORD
UNIVERSITY PRESS

S The News Room

Lesson 1

1 Listen and sing. 1.01 Watch!

2 Listen and repeat. 1.02

Welcome to River Town News! My name's Amy. What's your name?
My name's Lily.
I'm Joe.
My name's Charlie.

Sunday
Monday
Tuesday
Wednesday
Thursday
Friday
SCHOOL
Saturday

Hi! I'm Stella.

3 Listen and repeat. 1.03

4 Listen and number. 1.04

5 Write. What day is it today? Circle.

Sunday ______	T ______
M ______	F ______
T ______	S ______
W ______	
	Notes:

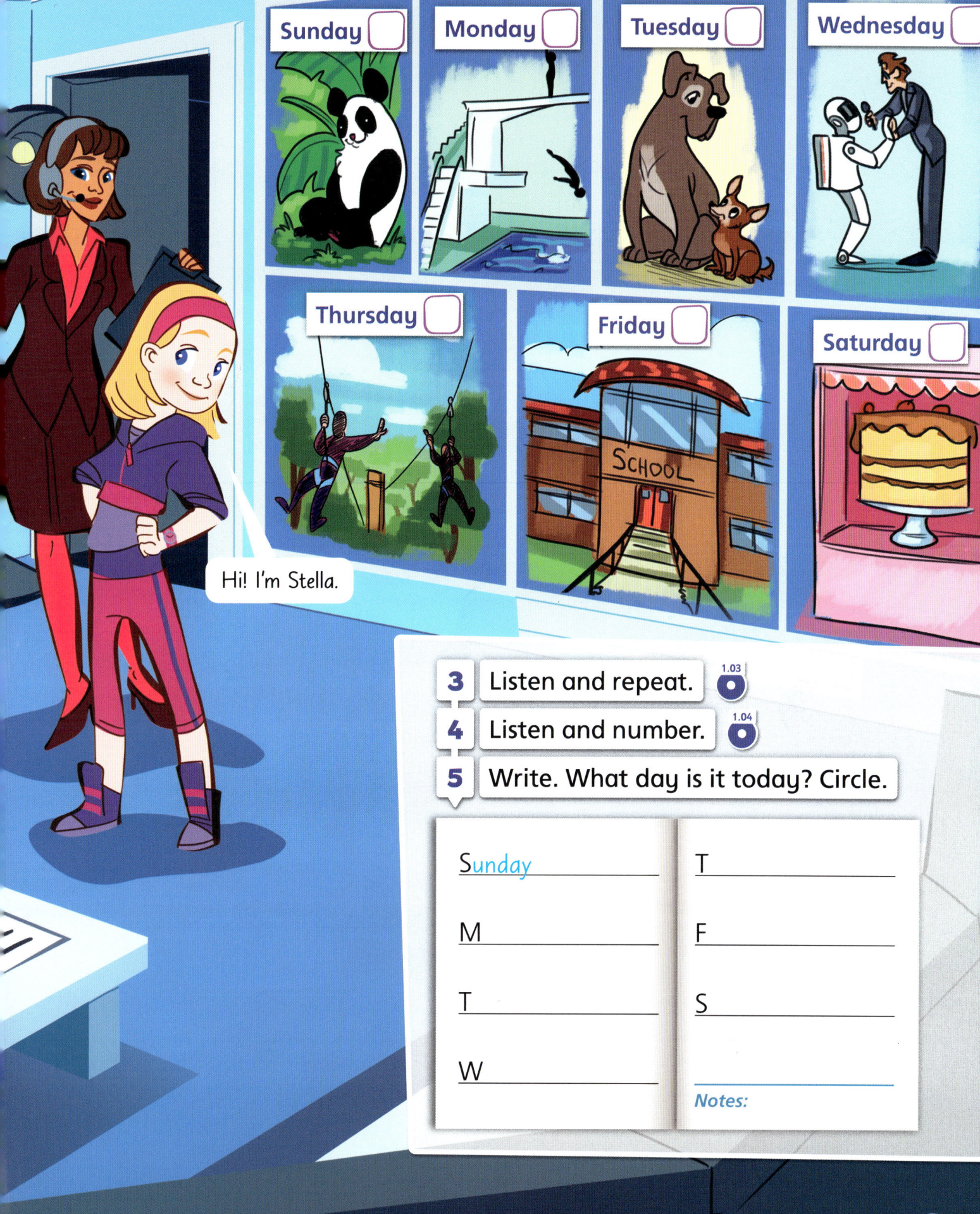

S Lesson 2

The News Team!

1 Listen and read. 1.05 Can you read the message? Act it out.

1
This is the news room.
Wow! An astronaut!
2
What's his name?
His name's Matt.
3
What's her job?
She's a pilot! There's the news helicopter.
4
And here are your desks! Welcome to the News Team. You're the Junior Crew.
Thanks!
5
I have a message.
Me too!
6
Me too. But I can't read it.

Find the jobs in the story. How many more jobs do you know?

Learn Grammar

What's her name?
Her name's Leila.
What's his name?
His name's Matt.

2 Listen and repeat. 1.06 Which question and answer is in the story?

3 Read and match. Write ***His*** or ***Her***. Ask and answer.

1		What's her name?	________ name's Amy.
2		What's her name?	________ name's Charlie.
3		What's his name?	________ name's Joe.
4		What's her name?	________ name's Stella.
5		What's his name?	________ name's Lily.

1 Sports News!

Lesson 1

1 Listen and repeat. 1.07

2 Listen and number. 1.08

surf
play soccer
play basketball
ride a bike
skateboard
play baseball

play volleyball
play tennis
Hi, Stella! Find out more about sports!

3 Write. Which sport can you do? Make a ✓.

1 

____

2 

____

3 

____

4 

____

5 

____

6 

____

7 

____

8 

____

4 Tell your friend.

I can ride a bike and I can skateboard. I can't surf!

1 Lesson 2

Go Charlie!

1 Listen and read. 1.09 What can Charlie do? Act it out.

1
RIVER TOWN GAMES
Wow! She can skateboard!
Look. There's baseball and tennis today.
EVENTS
2
Help! I can't stop!
12
3
My foot.
Oh no! The race! Can she ride?
No, she can't.
4
Wait a minute! I have an idea!
That's Amelia Angel!
12
5
Can he ride a bike?
Yes, he can!
6
Wow! He can ride a bike! Go Charlie!
12

How many sports can you see in the story? How many more do you know?

Learn Grammar

Can she ride a bike?
Can he ride a bike?
No, she can't.
Yes, he can.

2 Listen and repeat. 1.10 Underline the questions and answers in the story.

3 Read and match. Ask and answer.

1 

Can she skateboard? • • No, she can't.

2 

Can he play tennis? • • Yes, she can.

3 

Can she surf? • • Yes, he can.

4 

Can he play baseball? • • No, he can't.

HELP THE JUNIOR CREW! Find a blue T-shirt in the story. Draw what's on it. Now go to page 120.

Grammar Can she ride a bike? No, she can't. Yes, she can.

1 Lesson 3

1 Listen and repeat. 1.11 What's your favorite activity?

write stories

draw pictures

take photos

make videos

2 Listen and number. 1.12 Listen again and say the names.

3 Find, circle, and write.

jldtakephotoskgaimakevideoskawritestorieslanfdrawpictureshgs

1 ______________________

2 ______________________

3 ______________________

4 ______________________

Learn Grammar

Charlie, can you draw pictures?
Yes, I can!
Can you make videos?
No, I can't!

4 Listen and repeat. 1.13

5 Listen and make a ✓ or an ✗ for Joe. 1.14 Ask and answer about you.

6 Listen and sing. 1.15 Watch!

Song!

Tell me, tell me. Can Kate surf?
Let's make a video! Oh, oh!
No, no, no. No, she can't.
Don't make a video! No, no!
Tell me, Kate. Can you skateboard?
Let's make a video! Is that OK?
Yes, I can. Oh yes, I can.
Let's make a video. That's OK!

Tell me, tell me. Can Spike rock climb?
Let's make a video! Oh, oh!
No, no, no. No, he can't.
Don't make a video! No, no!
Tell me, Spike. Can you ride a bike?
Let's make a video! Is that OK?
Yes, I can. Oh yes, I can.
Let's make a video. Yeah, OK!

Grammar Can you draw pictures? Yes, I can. No, I can't.

Practice Page 99

1 Look. Which picture is the text about?

1 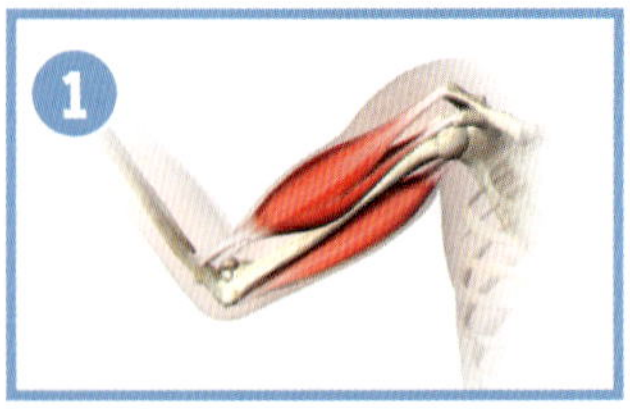
2 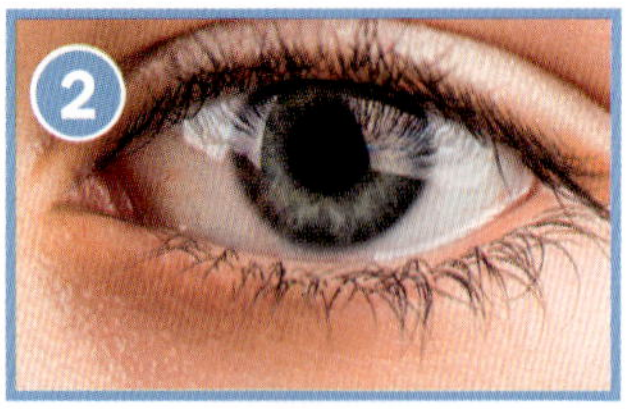
3 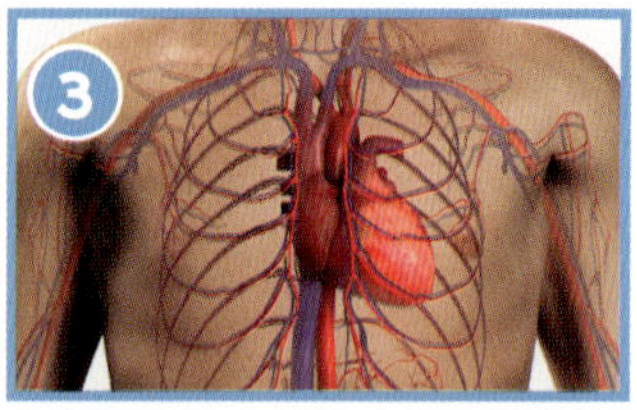
4 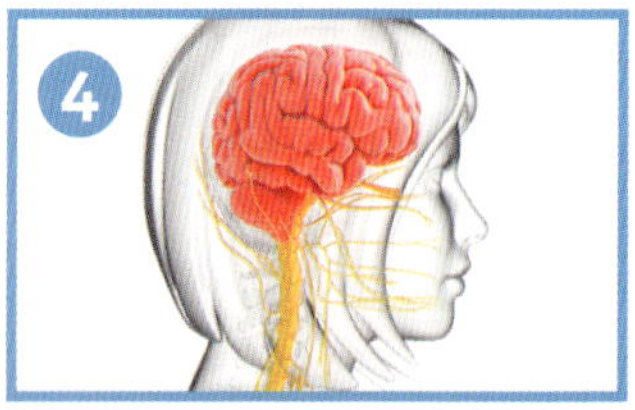

2 Read and listen. 1.16

Take Your Pulse!

pulse

Try this! Put your fingers on your arm. This is your **pulse**.

beat

seconds

Look at the clock. Can you count the **beats** for **15 seconds**?

Write the number. ☐

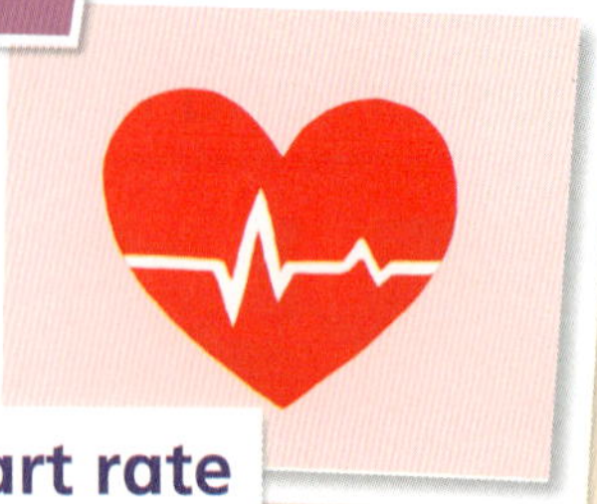

heart rate

Can you do the math?

4 x ☐ = ☐

That's your **heart rate** per **minute**.

Now run for two **minutes**. Count your pulse again. Is it the same or different?

02:00

minutes

3 Read and correct the mistakes.

1 Put your fingers on your ~~foot~~. _arm_

2 Count your pulse for twenty seconds. ________

3 Now run for five minutes. ________

4 Count your fingers again. ________

4 Do the Pulse Rate Experiment.

1 Lesson 5

1 Listen. 1.17 Who is the interview about? Make a √.

1 Two sisters. ☐ 2 A brother and a sister. ☐

2 Listen again and make a √ or an ✗. Ask and answer about Holly.

Holly

 ☐

 ☐

 ☐

 ☐

Everyday English!

3 Listen and repeat. 1.18

4 Act it out.

Can you surf?

Can you surf?	
√√√	Yes, I can. I can surf very well.
√	Yes, I can. I can surf well.
✗	No, I can't! I can't surf at all!

5 Make a Sports Hero poster. Ask and answer with a friend.

My Sports Hero
Novak Djokovic
He can play tennis very well!
This is Novak Djokovic. He can play tennis very well!
Can you play tennis?
Yes, I can. I can play well.

1 Lesson 6

1 Read and listen. 1.19 What's Amelia's favorite sport?

An interview with Amelia Angel – BMX superstar!

By Stella

12

Stella: Hi, Amelia! How are you?

Amelia: Fine, thank you!

Stella: Let's talk about sports. Can you surf?

Amelia: Yes, I can. I can surf very well!

Stella: Great! Can you skateboard?

Amelia: Yes, I can. I can skateboard very well.

Stella: And can you play tennis?

Amelia: No, I can't. I can't play tennis at all.

Stella: And what's your favorite sport?

Amelia: BMXing! I love it.

Stella: Of course! Amelia is our BMX champion!

Our Values Stella says: "We can all do sport! Find a new sport you can do!"

2 What can Amelia do? Read again and make a ✓, an ✗, or write ? for don't know.

3 What sport can you try? Go to the Values chart on page 119.

1 Review

1 Complete the puzzle. Who is it?

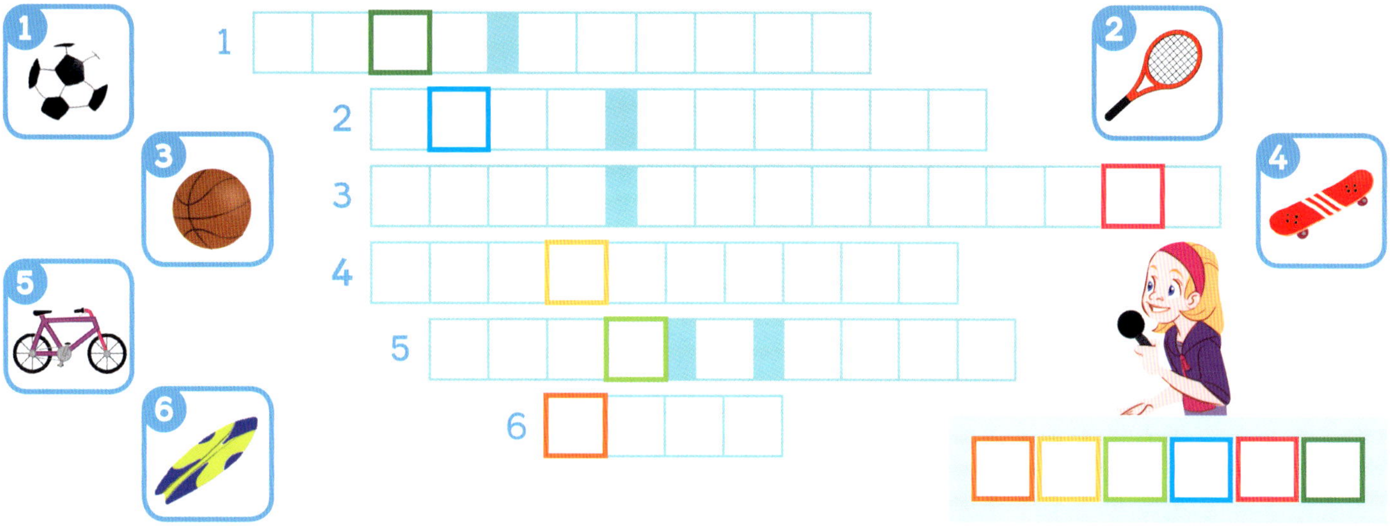

2 Write the words in order. Answer using ***Yes, I can.*** or ***No, I can't.***

1. tennis? play you Can ______________________ __________
2. you Can surf? ______________________ __________
3. you Can volleyball? play ______________________ __________
4. baseball? Can you play ______________________ __________

3 What can Joe do? Look and write.

☼	Ω	◊		∞	ә		≈	∫	Ω	↕	ә	☙	Δ	Ω	¥	●	
C				h			s	k		t		b	o		r	d	?

⊠	ә	≈		∞	ә		☼	Ω	◊	
Y			,		e			a	n	.

2 It's Showtime!

Lesson 1

1 Listen and repeat. 1.20

2 Listen and number. 1.21

secretary
acrobat
dancer
director
reporter
artist
CBI

builder
cleaner
Hi, Joe! Find out about shows!

3 Write. What do you want to be?

1 

2 

3 

4 

5 

6 

7 

8 

4 Tell your friend.

I want to be a reporter! I can write stories.

Two New Dancers!

1 Listen and read. 1.22 Can Lily dance? Act it out.

1
Here's the Junior Crew! They're reporters.
Welcome! It's the big night tonight!
2
Cool! Are they dancers?
No, they aren't. They're acrobats.
3
Are they artists?
Yes, they are.
4
Come on! Hurry up! All dancers over here!
5
Hurry up!
Wait! They aren't dancers!
They're reporters ...
6
Hey! Stella can dance! She's fantastic!
Yes, but Lily can't!

How many jobs can you see?
How many more do you know?

Learn Grammar

Are they dancers?

No, they aren't.
They aren't dancers. They're reporters!

2 Listen and repeat. 1.23 Find another question and answer in the story.

3 Read and match. Ask and answer.

1 

Are they reporters?

No, they aren't.

2 

Are they dancers?

3 

Are they artists?

Yes, they are.

4 

Are they directors?

HELP THE JUNIOR CREW! Find a red chair in the story. Draw what's on it. Now go to page 120.

2 Lesson 3

1 Listen and repeat. 1.24 When do you feel …?

excited

bored

afraid

proud

2 Read and circle.

1 

They're **bored** / **afraid**.

2 

They're **excited** / **proud**.

3 

They're **bored** / **excited**.

4 

They're **afraid** / **proud**.

3 Look and write.

1 ____________ 2 ____________ 3 ____________ 4 ____________

Learn Grammar

Are you afraid?
No, I'm not.
Yes, I am.

4 Listen and repeat. 1.25

5 Listen and number. 1.26

6 Listen and sing. 1.27 Watch!

Song!

It's showtime and I'm excited today!
Look at the acrobats, here at the show.
They aren't afraid, they aren't afraid.
I'm the director – I'm excited today!

It's showtime. We're here at the show!
It's showtime. It's showtime.
We're here at the show! It's showtime.

It's show time and I'm proud today!
Look at the chairs, here at the show.
They aren't dirty, they aren't dirty.
I'm the cleaner – I'm proud today!

It's showtime. We're here at the show!
It's showtime. It's showtime.
We're here at the show! It's showtime.

Grammar Are you afraid? No, I'm not. Yes, I am.

Practice Page 101

2 Lesson 4

Art

1 Look at the pictures. What are the feelings?

2 Read and listen. 1.28

Drawing cartoon faces

Can you draw **cartoon faces**? It's fun!

1 

Draw a circle.

2 

Draw three lines.

3 

Draw eyes, a nose and a mouth.

4 

Draw ears and hair!

5 Add some feelings:

They're **afraid**. Look at the eyes. The mouths are closed.

They're **surprised**. The eyes are big. The mouths are open.

They're **angry**. The eyes are closed. Look at the mouths.

3 Read and draw.

He's surprised. She's afraid. She's angry. He's happy.

4 Do the Cartoon Workshop worksheet.

2 Lesson 5

1 Listen. 1.29 Number the pictures.

2 Listen again and circle.

1 The acrobats aren't afraid. They're ... a bored. b angry. c excited.

2 The artists are ... a sad. b proud. c surprised.

3 The dancers are ... a happy. b excited. c surprised.

Everyday English!

3 Listen and repeat. 1.30

4 Look at the photos again and say.

Look at this photo. I think they're **acrobats**.

Really? I don't think so. I think they're **dancers**.

Yes, I think so, too.

5 Work in groups or pairs. Play a mime game.

Are you afraid?
No, I'm not.
Are you surprised?

1 Read and listen. 1.31 How many dancers are in the show?

Search...

Joe's Blog

Posts

What's New in River Town?

There's a new show in town. Are you excited? There are twenty dancers and twenty acrobats. They're stars! But there are lots of other people in the show. They're cleaners and builders and artists. Inside the building it is clean, and the decorations and pictures are beautiful! They work together and everyone is proud. Go and see this fantastic show!

Our Values Joe says: "Work together and be part of a team!"

2 Read again and circle ***Yes*** or ***No***.

1	There are twenty acrobats in the show.	Yes	No
2	You can see clowns in the show.	Yes	No
3	The cleaners are the stars.	Yes	No
4	You can see decorations.	Yes	No
5	The cleaners and builders and artists are proud.	Yes	No

3 When can you be part of a team? Go to the Values chart on page 119.

 Writing practice Page 101

2 Review

1 Find, circle, and write.

hgkdirectorjgaproudjgcleaneralborederemexcitedlsa

1 ______ 2 ______ 3 ______ 4 ______ 5 ______

2 Look and match. Write.

1 

2 

3 

4 

5 

A 

B 

C 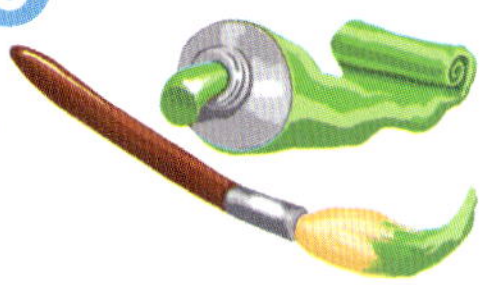

D 

E 

secretaries acrobats dancers cleaners ~~artists~~

1 (builders) They aren't builders. They're artists.

2 (directors) They ______ directors. They're ______

3 (cleaners) ______

4 (reporters) ______

5 (secretaries) ______

Popular Sports

1 Look at the pictures. What is the text about?

2 Listen and read. 1.32

3 Read again and circle ***Football*** or ***Hockey***.

4 Project! Make a poster about your favorite sport.

hockey

Can you play **hockey** or **football**? They are popular sports in the USA.

Hockey is a **team** game.

There are six **players** on a team. Hockey is fast and can be dangerous but the players aren't afraid! They're excited! The players have shorts, but it isn't hot – it's cold!

football
team

player

There are eleven players on a football team. The ball is big and long. Players can throw and catch the ball. They run fast. Children can play football at school.

1	There are six players.	**Football**	**Hockey**
2	The ball is big and long.	**Football**	**Hockey**
3	The players run fast.	**Football**	**Hockey**
4	This game can be dangerous.	**Football**	**Hockey**
5	You can play this at school.	**Football**	**Hockey**

My favorite sport is Ice Hockey!
My favorite player is Hilary Knight.
My favorite team is the Boston Blades
BOSTON 18
My favorite sport is hockey!
It's fun! I can play hockey.
My favorite team is Boston Blades.

Exchange!

What are popular sports in your country? Can you play them?

3 In the Ocean

Lesson 1

1 Listen and repeat. 1.33

2 Listen and number. 1.34

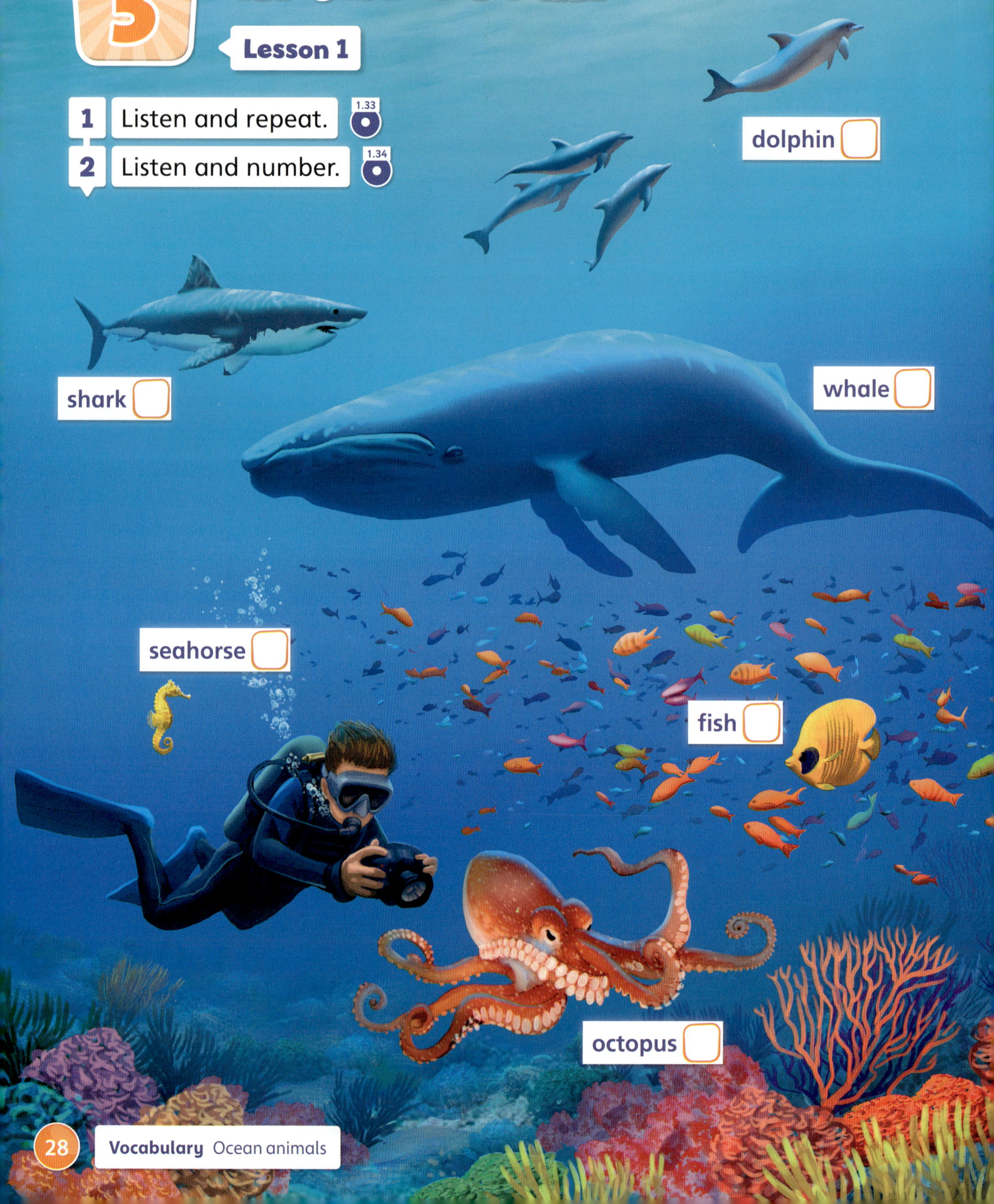
dolphin
shark
whale
seahorse
fish
octopus

seal
turtle
Hi, Lily! Find out about ocean animals!

3 Write. Which is your favorite animal?

1 

____

2 

____

3 

____

4 

____

5 

____

6 

____

7 

____

8 

____

4 Tell your friend.

What's your favorite animal?
My favorite animal is a dolphin. It can swim and jump!

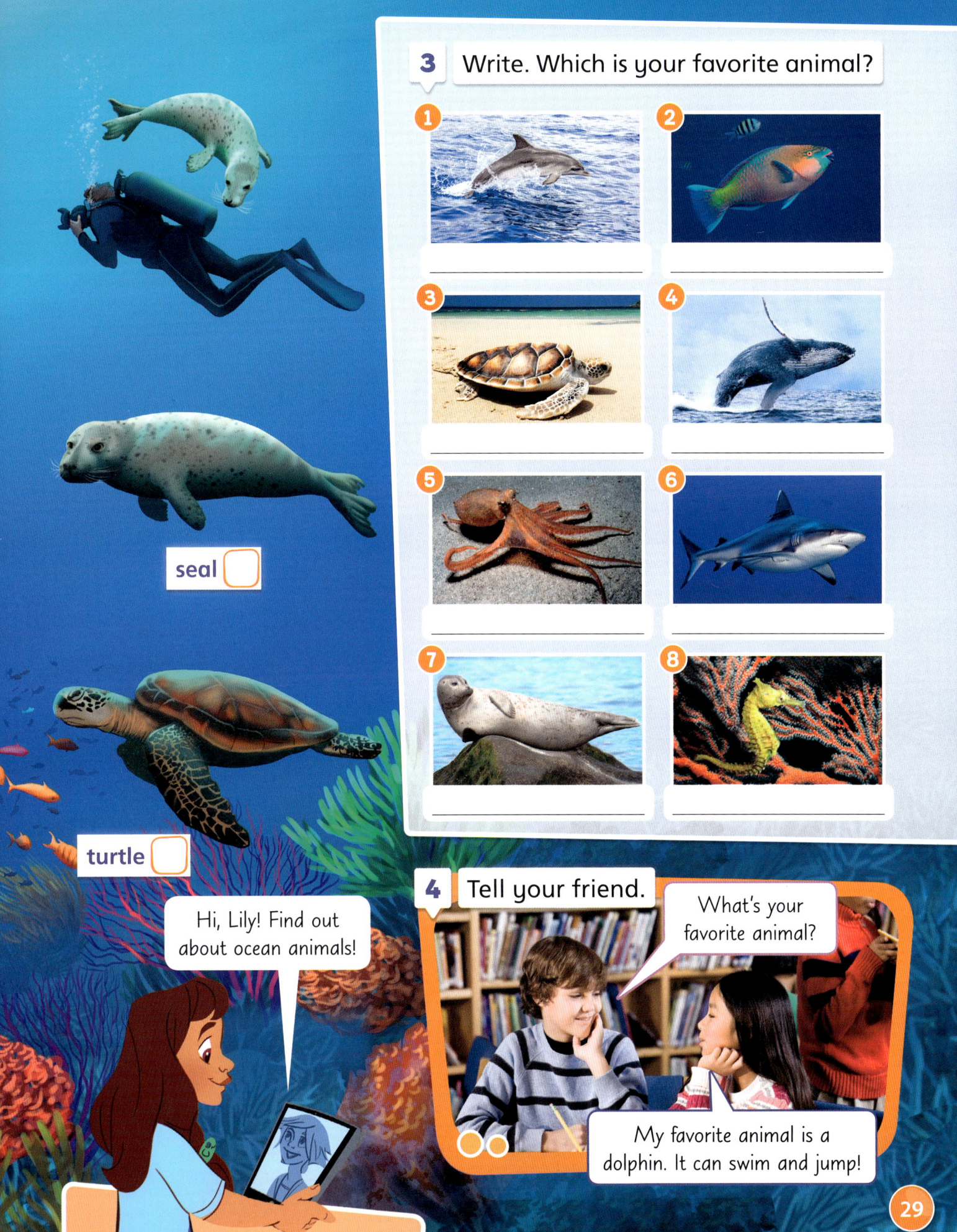

3 Lesson 2

Beach Rescue!

1 Listen and read. 1.35 Why are the dolphins excited? Act it out.

1
Look! This is a fish!
Cool! And these are gray seals.
2
Wow! These are dolphins!
That's strange! They're next to the beach ...
3
These dolphins are excited.
I don't understand. What's wrong?
4
Look! It can't swim.
Hello! Can you help?
5
This dolphin is OK.
Good job, kids!
6
They're all happy now!

How many animals can you see?
How many more do you know?

Learn Grammar

This is a fish.  These are seals. 

2 Listen and repeat. 1.36 How many seals are there? How many fish?

3 Read and circle. Match and say.

1 
an octopus / octopuses

2 
seahorses / a seahorse

This is

These are

3 
sharks / a shark

4 
a turtle / turtles

5 
a fish / fish

6 
dolphins / a dolphin

HELP THE JUNIOR CREW!

Find a boat in the story. Draw what's on it. Now go to page 120.

3 Lesson 3

1 Listen and repeat. 1.37 What are you like? Make a ✓.

friendly ☐

funny ☐

smart ☐

shy ☐

2 Read and match. Listen and check. 1.38

1 These dolphins are	funny.	They can hide.
2 These seahorses are	friendly.	It can do puzzles.
3 This octopus is	shy.	It can catch fish!
4 This seal is	smart.	They can play with friends.

3 Unscramble the words and write.

1 s r t a m ______

2 y s h ______

3 d l f i e r n y ______

4 n n y u f ______

Learn Grammar

What's that?
What are those?
That's a shark!
Those are whales.

4 Listen and repeat. 1.39

5 Circle five different animals! Listen and check. 1.40

6 Listen and sing. 1.41 Watch!

Song!

Ocean safari! This is fun! Ocean safari! Look! What are those?
Those are dolphins. They're friendly. Ocean safari! This is fun!
Ocean safari! This is fun! Ocean safari! Look! What's that?
That's a seahorse. Oh, it's shy. Ocean safari! This is fun!
Ocean safari! This is fun! Ocean safari! Look! What are those?
Those are seals. Oh, they're funny. Ocean safari! This is fun!

Ocean safari! This is fun! Ocean safari! Look! What's that?
That's a shark. A shark? Oh no! Ocean safari! Quick! Let's go!

Grammar What's that? That's a shark. What are those? Those are whales.

Practice Page 103

1 Look at the picture. How many *zones* are there?

2 Read and listen. 1.42

Ocean habitats

A **habitat** is a home. The ocean has many different habitats! Look, there are three different zones in the ocean.

A
B
C
rock pool

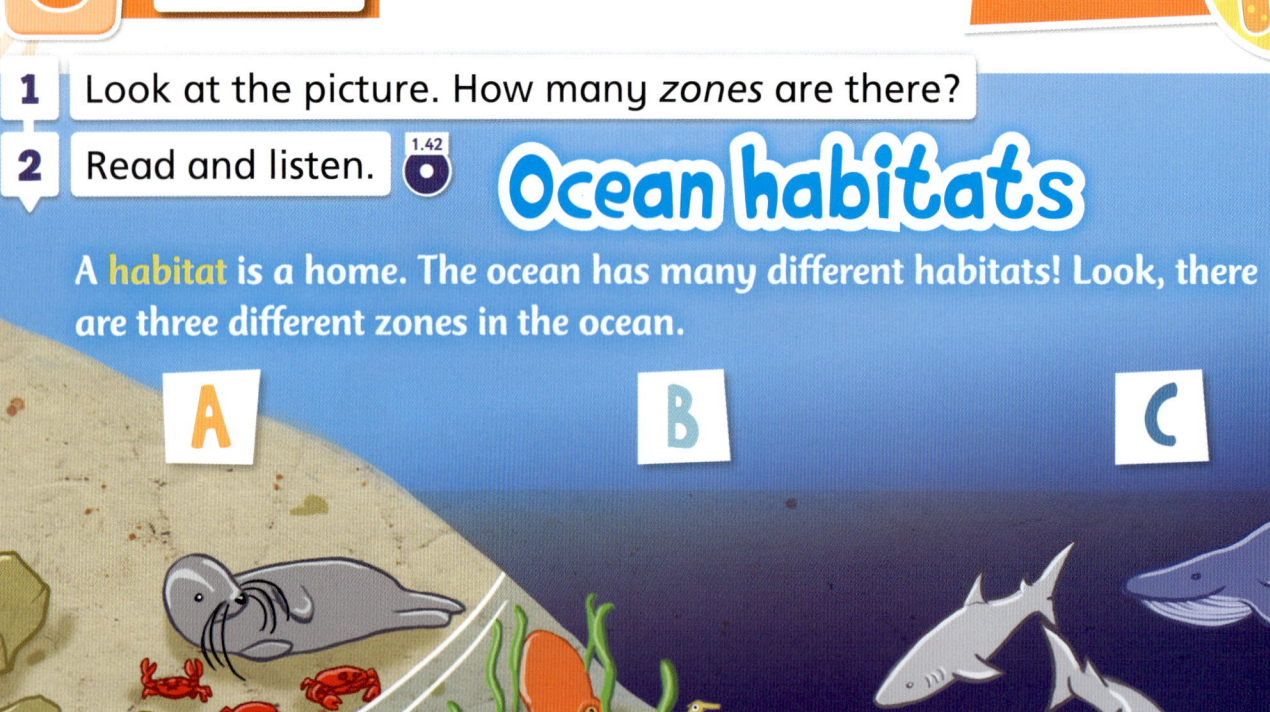

The **beach** is wet and dry. Crabs and seals are here. They can go in the water, too. Crabs like the **rock pools**.

Shallow water is warm. This octopus is on the **ocean floor**. Seahorses are here, too.

The ocean is **deep**. You can find sharks and whales here. They can swim a long way.

3 Look and write the animals in the correct list.

A	B	C
______	______	______
______	______	______

4 Do the Ocean Habitats worksheet.

3 Lesson 5

1 Listen. 1.43 Point to the animals.

2 Listen again and draw the path.

ICE CREAM

Everyday English!

3 Listen and repeat. 1.44

4 Act it out.

have an ice cream
see the sharks
climb a tree
see the octopuses

What next?

Let's go and see the dolphins next.

5 Make an Ocean Collage. Talk about your picture.

Look! Those are dolphins.
And this is an octopus.

1 Read and listen. 1.45 Can you solve the puzzles?

Lily's Nature Puzzles

Ocean animals

A

These animals are big and smart. They're shy, too. They like deep water. They can't run but they can swim and jump. They can dive!

Here's some help:

What's this? 

Listen to this.

What are they? ______________

B

These animals are big! They aren't very friendly, they're shy! They like the water. They can swim and they can walk on the beach.

Here's some help:

What are these? 

Look! This is home. 

What are they? ______________

Our Values Lily says: "Respect nature! Take care of the ocean!"

2 Read again and write ***A*** or ***B***.

1 This animal is smart. ☐
2 This animal has four legs. ☐
3 This animal can jump and dive. ☐
4 This animal can walk. ☐
5 This animal can sing. ☐
6 You can see this animal on the beach. ☐

3 How can you take care of the ocean? Go to the Values chart on page 119.

 Writing practice Page 103

3 Review

1 What animal is it? Write.

seahorse dolphin octopus shark turtle

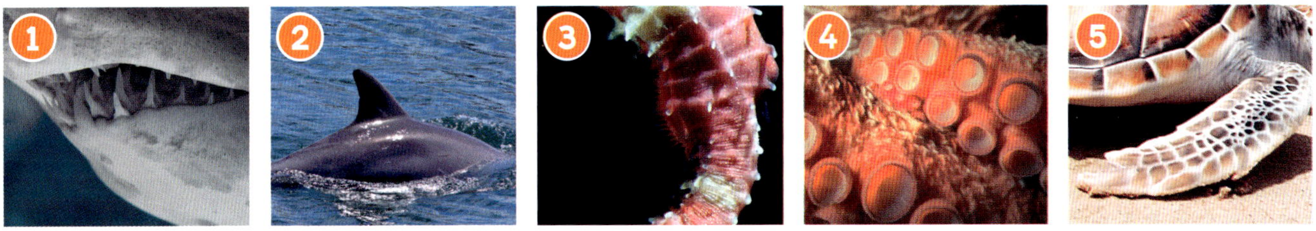
1
2
3
4
5

1 ____________ 2 ____________ 3 ____________ 4 ____________ 5 ____________

2 Look and write *This*, *That*, *These*, or *Those*.

1 ________ dolphins are fast!
2 ________ dolphins are friendly!
3 ________ whale is big!
4 ________ whale is shy!

3 Choose and draw animals. Write.

those whales fish seals these octopuses

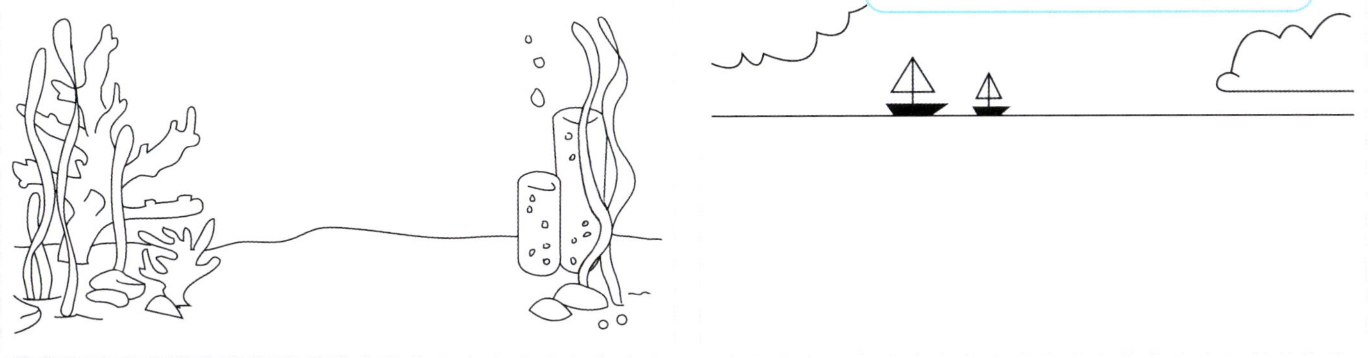

1 What are ____________? ____________.

2 What are ____________? ____________.

4 At the Fun Run!

Lesson 1

1 Listen and repeat. 1.46

2 Listen and number. 1.47

cap
GREAT JOB!!!
umbrella
money
medal
costume
first aid kit

water bottle
backpack
Hi, Charlie! Find out about the people in our town!

3 Write. What's in your backpack? Make a ✓.

1 

____

2 

____

3 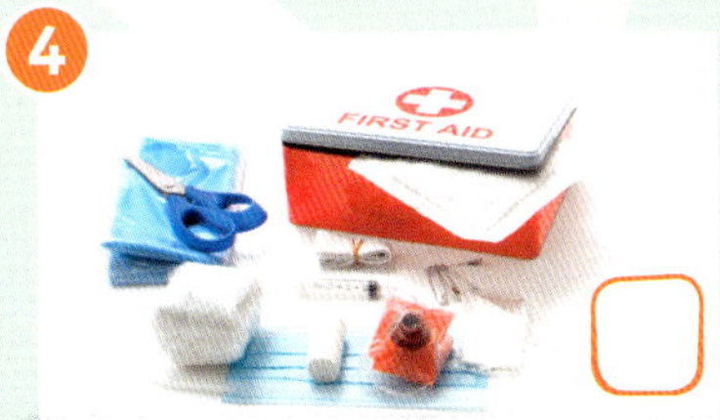
FIRST AID

____

4 

____

5 

____

6 

____

7 

____

8 

____

4 Tell your friend.

I have a cap and a water bottle. I don't have an umbrella!

4 Lesson 2

At the Fun Run

1 Listen and read. 1.48 What's Amy's costume? Act it out.

FUN RUN
1
I can't see Amy.
2
Does she have an umbrella?
No, she doesn't. That isn't Amy.
3
Does she have a pink cap?
No, she doesn't.
4
There's Amy! She has an astronaut costume!
Cool! And there's her brother.
5
Wow! You have a lot of money, Amy!
Yes! It's heavy!
6
This is great for the new playground.
Thank you, Amy! Here's your medal!

How many useful things are in the story? Make a list.

Learn Grammar

Does he have a water bottle?
Does she have a pink cap?
Yes, he does.
No, she doesn't.

2 Listen and repeat. 1.49 Which question is in the story? Underline another question and answer.

3 Find them in the story. Read and make a ✓. Ask and answer.

1 

Does he have a water bottle?

Yes, he does. ☐ No, he doesn't. ☐

2 

Does he have a medal?

Yes, he does. ☐ No, he doesn't. ☐

3 

Does he have a backpack?

Yes, he does. ☐ No, he doesn't. ☐

4 

Does she have an umbrella?

Yes, she does. ☐ No, she doesn't. ☐

HELP THE JUNIOR CREW!

Find an umbrella in the story. Draw what's on it. Now go to page 120.

4 Lesson 3

1 Listen and repeat. 1.50 Which other family words do you know?

aunt

uncle

cousins

friends

2 Listen and make a ✓ or an ✗. 1.51

	aunts	uncles	cousins	friends
Amy	☐	☐	☐	☐
Joe	☐	☐	☐	☐

Amy

Joe

3 How many? Read and write.

uncles cousins aunts

1 My mom has three sisters. I have ___three___ __________.

2 My mom has three brothers and my dad has two brothers.
I have __________ __________.

3 My cousin has two sisters. I have __________ __________.

Learn Grammar

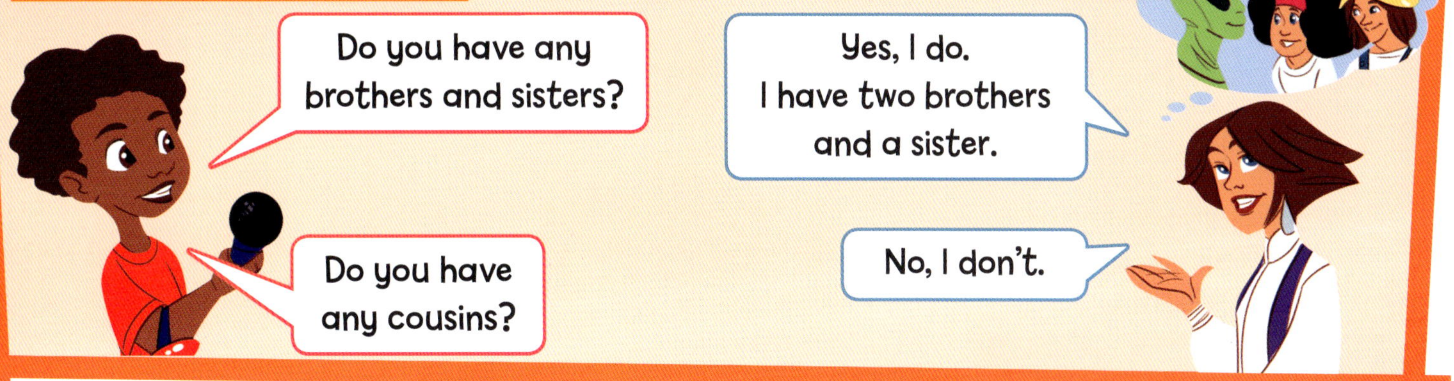

Do you have any brothers and sisters?
Yes, I do. I have two brothers and a sister.
Do you have any cousins?
No, I don't.

4 Listen and repeat. 1.52

5 Listen and number. 1.53 Ask and answer for you.

12
21

HAPPY BIRTHDAY

6 Listen and sing. 1.54 Watch!

Song!

Do you have, do you have any aunts?
Yes, I do. I have two: Aunt Anne and Aunt Fran.
Do you have, do you have any uncles?
Yes, I do. I have two: Uncle Tim and Uncle Jim.

Do you have, do you have any cousins?
Yes, I do. I have ten: Joey and Zoe, Lee and Marie,
Jamie and Amy, Billy and Lily, Ricky and Nikki.
Ten cousins! Ten cousins! Ten cousins and we're friends!

Grammar Do you have any cousins? Yes, I do. No, I don't.

Practice Page 105

1 Look. How many safe sport ideas can you see?

2 Read and listen. 1.55

Safe Sports

Sports are good for you – and here are five ideas to help you stay safe.

1 Stay cool. Is it sunny? Put on your cap.

2 **Warm up** your **muscles**. Jump and **jog** for three minutes.

muscle

3 Drink water! Do you have a water bottle?

4 **Take a break** and have a healthy snack!

5 **Stretch** after sports. Stretch your muscles in your arms and legs.

3 Read and number.

1. He has a water bottle. ☐
2. He has a cap. ☐
3. She can jog. ☐
4. He can stretch. ☐
5. Have an orange for a snack. ☐

4 Do the Safe Sports Journal worksheet.

4 Lesson 5

1 Listen. 1.56 Number the pictures.

SPORTS DAY

2 Listen again and match.

1
2
3
4
5
6
Picnic
Sports Day
Fun Run

Everyday English!

library beach party | your friends money

Let's go to the **fun run**!

What shall I bring?

Bring **a water bottle** and **a cap**.

3 Listen and repeat. 1.57

4 Act it out.

5 Choose an event. Make a checklist with six useful things. Play the game.

Family picnic
salad
Fun Run
cap
water bottle
costume
money
snack
Do you have a water bottle?
Yes, I do.

4 Lesson 6

1 Read and listen. 1.58 What is Amy's job?

People in town:

A fun runner!

By Charlie

Amy is a reporter, but for one day she's an astronaut! Today is the Fun Run. The run is for the playground.

Amy has her astronaut costume. She has a water bottle and a backpack, too.

Her two brothers, sister, two aunts, and lots of friends are also in the fun run.

Amy has a medal. She has lots of money, too. Now the town can have a new playground!

94
52
55

Our Values Charlie says: "It's important to help people!"

2 Read again and write the answers.

Yes, she does. No, she doesn't.

1 Does Amy have a first aid kit? ____________________

2 Does she have an acrobat costume? ____________________

3 Does she have a backpack? ____________________

4 Does she have five brothers? ____________________

5 Does she have a medal? ____________________

6 Does she have lots of money? ____________________

3 How can you help your family and friends? Go to the Values chart on page 119.

Writing practice Page 105

4 Review

1 Look and write.

aunt uncle cousins ~~grandma~~ grandpa sister mom dad

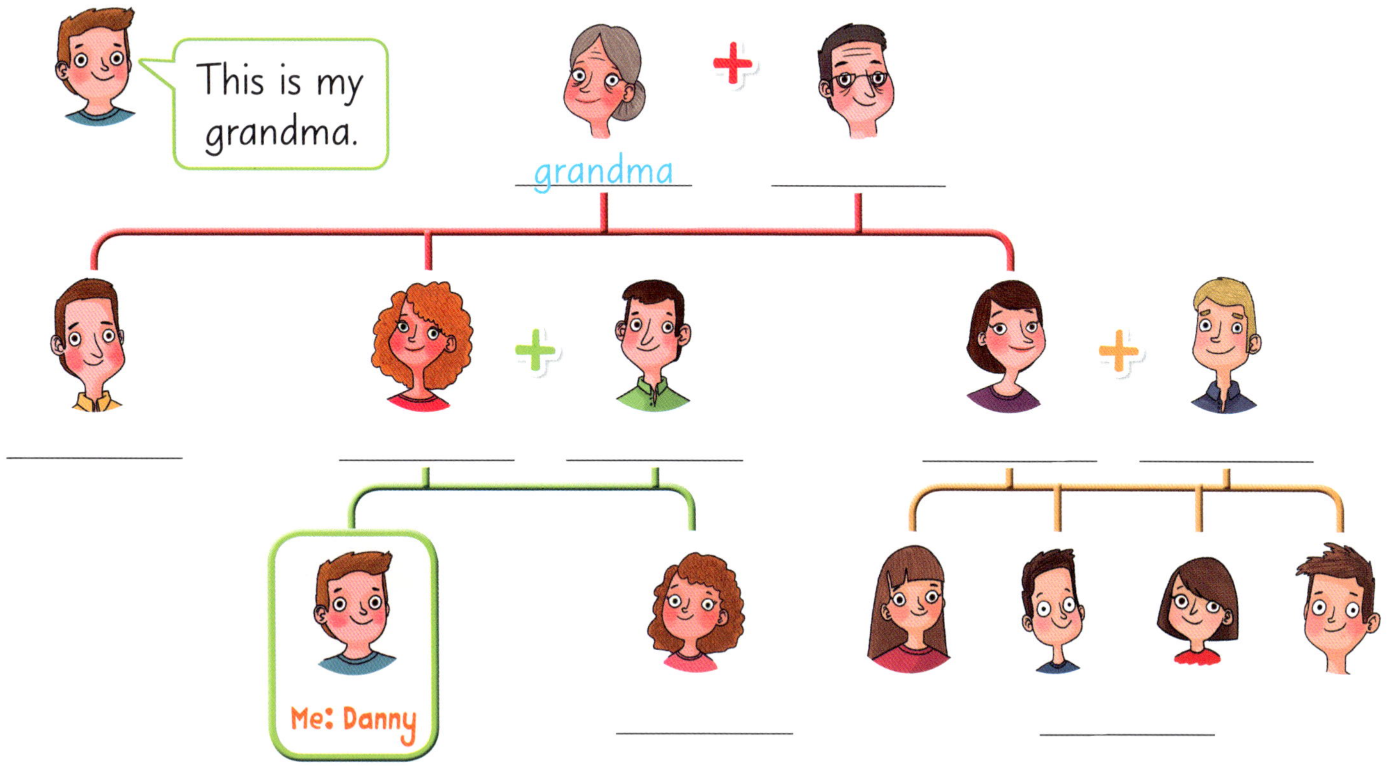
This is my grandma.
grandma
Me: Danny

2 Look at activity 1 again. Complete the interview with Danny.

Do you have any brothers and sisters?

Yes, I do. I have a sister.

Do you have ________ any uncles?

Yes, ________________. I have two uncles.

____

Yes, ________________. ________________ one aunt.

____

________________. ________________ four cousins.

Culture 2 Out in the Wild!

1 Look at the pictures. What is the text about?

2 Listen and read. 1.59

3 Read again and write ***Yes*** or ***No***.

4 Project! Make a leaflet for the national park.

rainforest

Greetings from
Legend of Bigfoot

postcard

The northwestern USA is beautiful. Here is the *Olympic National Park*. It is next to the Pacific Ocean where you can see whales and dolphins. There's a big **rainforest** with huge trees. There are also lots of old stories!

People say there's a **monster** in the rainforest. His name is Bigfoot. He's famous!

There are **postcards** and **souvenirs** of Bigfoot in the stores.

souvenirs

LEGEND OF
BIGFOOT

Bigfoot is shy! Nobody can find him. This is a photo of Bigfoot, but is he real? Maybe he's a big bear. Maybe he's a real monster or maybe it's just a story.

monster

1 You can see whales and dolphins in the rainforest. ________

2 The stories are about a monster. ________

3 The monster lives in the rainforest. ________

4 There are Bigfoot souvenirs. ________

5 Bigfoot is friendly. ________

You can see whales and dolphins!
Bring a cap and a waterbottle.
The Olympic National Park
Things to see
Things to bring
sea otters
birds
whales
mountains
rainforest
fish
money
packed lunch
water
cap
water bottle
first aid kit

Exchange!

Do you know any other stories about strange animals or monsters?

5 At the Fashion Show

Lesson 1

1. Listen and repeat. 1.60
2. Listen and number. 1.61

shirt ☐

coat ☐

jeans ☐

sneakers ☐

sandals ☐

Fashion Week

scarf ☐
dress ☐
leggings ☐

3 Write. Which clothes can you see in the classroom? Make a ✓.

1. ☐ _____ 
2. ☐ _____ 
3. ☐ _____ 
4. ☐ _____ 
5. ☐ _____ 
6. ☐ _____ 
7. ☐ _____ 
8. ☐ _____ 

Hi, Stella! Find out about clothes and fashion!

4 Play a game. Who is it?

I can see a red dress.

It's Anna!

Yes. Your turn!

5 Lesson 2 Old and New

1 Listen and read. 1.62 Why are the clothes in the show blue? Act it out.

1
It's the fashion show tonight. Are you excited?
Yes! Look. Here are the clothes.
2
Oh no! These aren't my clothes!
3
Can I see the pictures, please?
Oh Stella! You can do it!
4
Oh! She isn't wearing a pink dress.
5
Look! She's wearing sandals.
Wow! He's wearing a cool scarf and shirt!
6
Thank you everyone! And thank you Stella!
Old jeans are cool now!

Which clothes do you know in the story? Do you know any more?

Learn Grammar

She isn't wearing a pink dress.
She's wearing a blue dress.

2 Listen and repeat. 1.63 Underline the sentence which is in the story.

3 Find them in the story. Match and say.

1 

A 

She's wearing sandals.

2 

B 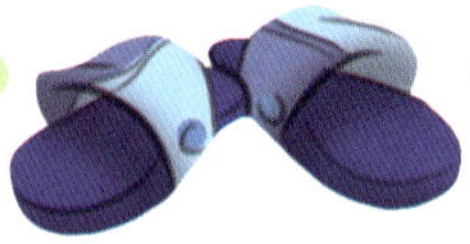

He's wearing a scarf.

3 

C 

She's wearing a dress.

4 

D 

She's wearing a shirt.

HELP THE JUNIOR CREW! Find a dress in the story. Draw what's on it. Now go to page 120.

1 Listen and repeat. 1.64 What do you have? Make a √.

sunglasses ☐

gloves ☐

watch ☐

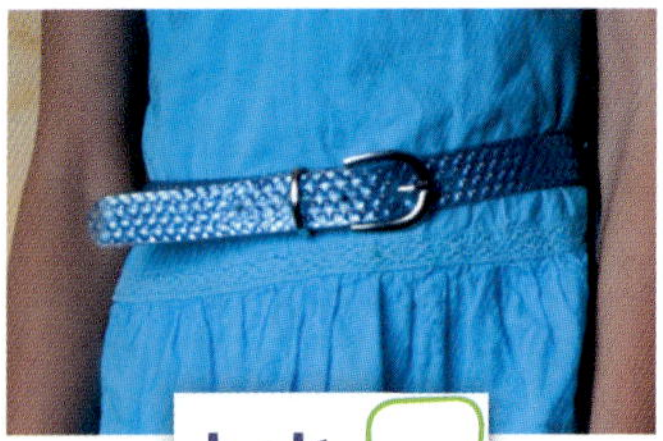
belt ☐

2 Listen and number. 1.65

3 Complete the puzzle. Draw what's in the bag.

1

2

3

4

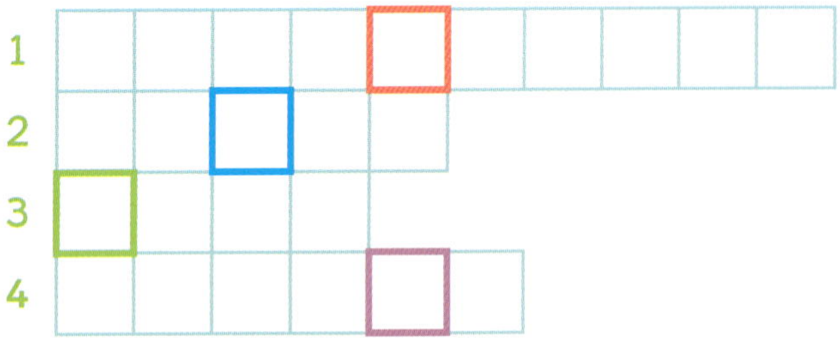
1
2
3
4

Learn Grammar

What's he wearing?
He's wearing sunglasses.

4 Listen and repeat. 1.66

5 Listen and number. 1.67 Play the game.

What's he wearing?
A watch and sunglasses.
2

6 Listen and sing. 1.68 Watch!

Song!

Look at Cassie on the cool catwalk.
What's she wearing? She's wearing gloves.
Look at Caspar on the cool catwalk.
What's he wearing? He's wearing jeans.

Look at Carla on the cool catwalk.
What's she wearing? She's wearing a belt.
Look at Conor on the cool catwalk.
What's he wearing? He's wearing a watch.
Look at us, we're on the cool catwalk!

Grammar What's he wearing? He's wearing sunglasses.

Practice Page 107

1 Look at the title and the pictures. What's special about these clothes?

2 Read and listen. 1.69

Old things, new things!

Do you have any old jeans? Do you have any old bags or paper? Don't put them in the **trash can**.

You can **recycle** them. Look at these cool ideas!

Look at this bag. It's **made of** old jeans!

She's wearing a dress. It's made of old potato chip bags! Look at all the cool colors.

He's wearing a hat. It's made of old paper!

What can you **design**? What can you recycle?

3 Read and match the sentence halves.

1. The dress is made of
2. The bag is made of
3. The hat is made of
4. All the things are made of
5. You can recycle to make

- old paper.
- different kinds of trash.
- potato chip bags.
- cool new clothes.
- old jeans.

4 Do the Recycled Design worksheet.

5 Lesson 5

1 Listen. 1.70 What's the sister's name?

2 Listen again and number the four models they talk about.

Everyday English!

blue/pink jeans/leggings sneakers/sandals

3 Listen and repeat. 1.71

4 Act it out.

I love purple!

Really? I prefer red.

5 Make a Mixed-up Fashion Model. Talk about your picture.

belt
scarf
gloves
dress
leggings

sunglasses
shirt
watch
jeans
gloves
sandals

He's wearing blue jeans and a pink shirt. He's wearing big sunglasses!

5 Lesson 6

1 Read and listen. 1.72 How many *looks* are in Stella's text?

Stella's Fashion Page!

What are your favorite clothes? What's your look?

Sporty!

You like sports and games!

Look, he's wearing shorts, a T-shirt, and sneakers. He's wearing gloves, too. She's wearing a pink sweater and leggings. Look at her watch!

Cool!

You like fashion and music!

This boy is wearing jeans with boots. He's wearing sunglasses, too! And she's wearing a very cool coat and a scarf.

Stylish!

You like parties!

She's wearing a blue dress and sandals. Look at her belt! He's wearing stylish pants with a jacket and a white shirt.

Our Values Stella says: "We are all different. Choose your own look!"

2 Read again and write the answers.

1 She's sporty. What's she wearing? ____________________

2 He's cool. What's he wearing? ____________________

3 She's fashionable. What's she wearing? ____________________

3 How are you and your friends the same and different? Go to the Values chart on page 119.

5 Review

1 Look and write.

T-shirt jeans ~~sunglasses~~ sandals
leggings shirt sneakers cap

sunglasses / ______

______ / ______

______ / ______

______ / ______

2 Follow and complete.

1 What's she wearing? She's wearing ______.

2 ______? He's ______.

3 ______

3 Write sentences. Read and number the correct picture.

1 ✗ she / leggings She isn't wearing leggings.

2 ✗ he / jeans ______

3 ✗ she / sunglasses ______

4 ✗ he / sneakers ______

6 At the Wildlife Club

Lesson 1

1 Listen and repeat. 2.01

2 Listen and number. 2.02

listen
sleep
build
watch
drink
read
eat

walk

3 Write. Where can you do these actions? Write some ideas!

1 

____

2 

____

3 

____

4 

____

5 

____

6 

____

7 

____

8 

____

Hi, Lily! Find out more about wildlife!

4 Ask and answer.

Where can you sleep?
In a tent!
Yes. OK, your turn!

6 Lesson 2

A Wild Idea!

1 Listen and read. 2.03 Are the animals safe? Act it out.

1 On Saturday.
Look down there! They're from the Wildlife Club.
2
But what is it?
They're building something.
3 On Tuesday.
Look! It's a tunnel. It's really big!
4
Come and look inside!
The animals can go in the tunnel. It's safe.
5
It's nighttime, but they aren't sleeping.
Look! They're drinking.
6
Yay! They're walking in the tunnel!
They're safe!

How many action words can you find in the story?

Learn Grammar

They aren't sleeping.
They're drinking.

2 Listen and repeat. 2.04 Underline these sentences in the story.

3 Find six differences. Read and write ***A*** or ***B***. Listen and check. 2.05

A

B

1  They aren't building. ☐

2  They aren't drinking. ☐

3  They aren't listening. ☐

4  They're eating. ☐

5  They're watching. ☐

6  They're sleeping. ☐

HELP THE JUNIOR CREW! Find a tree in the story. Draw what's on it. Now go to page 120.

6 Lesson 3

1 Listen and repeat. 2.06 Do you have a watch like this?

quarter to six | six o'clock | quarter past six | six thirty

2 Look, read, and number.

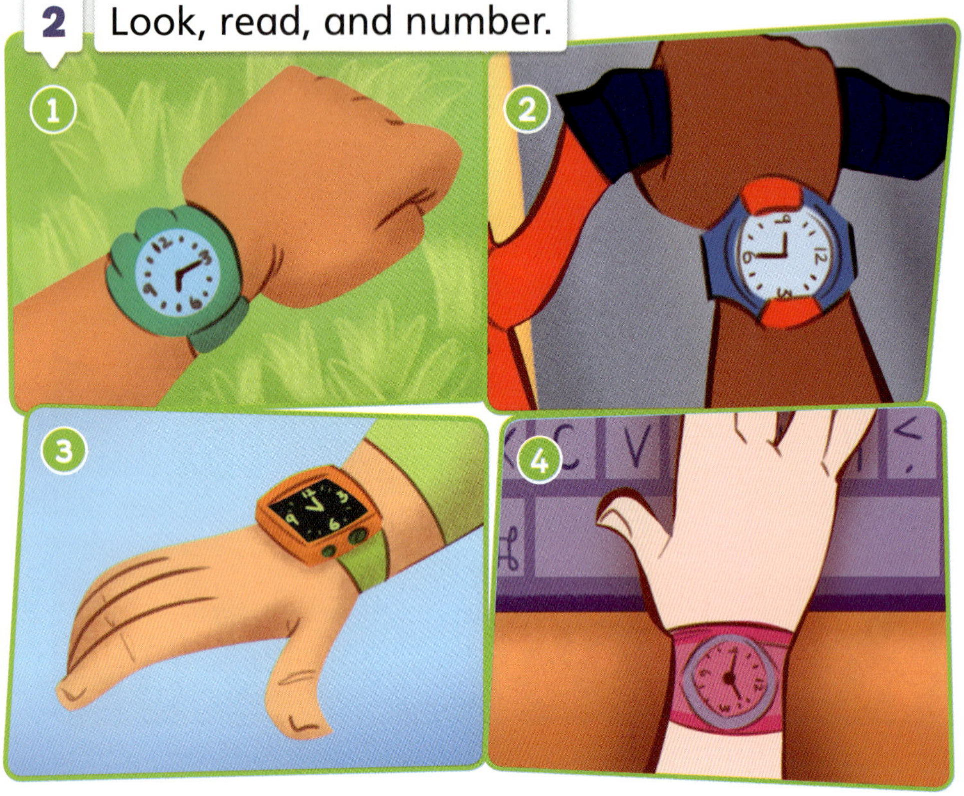

1
2
3
4

☐ It's nine thirty.

☐ It's quarter to two.

☐ It's eleven o'clock.

☐ It's quarter past seven.

3 Complete and match.

1 q__a___e__ ___ th____

2 o___ t__i___y

3 ___a__t__r __a__t _____

4 s__v___ o'___oc__

A
B
C
D

Learn Grammar

What time is it?
It's quarter to two.

4 Listen and repeat. 2.07

5 Listen and make a ✓. 2.08 Ask and answer.

6 Listen and sing. 2.09 Watch

Song!

What time is it? It's eleven o'clock.
It's nighttime now, but my sisters aren't sleeping.
It's twelve o'clock. It's one o'clock.
It's nighttime now, but my sisters aren't sleeping.
It's two o'clock, it's three o'clock, it's four o'clock,
but they aren't sleeping.
They're listening to all their favorite songs.
Awake at night and tired in the day! Awake at night!
Awake at night and tired in the day! Awake at night!
(Repeat)

74
74

Grammar What time is it? It's quarter to two.

Practice Page 109

1 Look at the pictures. What are the bears doing?

2 Read and listen. 2.10

seasons

Four seasons with the bears

These are grizzly bears! They're big. In the USA, there are bears in the wild. Read about the bears in each **season** of the year.

It's **summer**. The young bears are playing. They're climbing and walking.

It's **fall**. The bears are eating. They're building, too.

It's **winter**. It's snowy outside. The bears aren't eating. They aren't drinking. They are sleeping inside their home.

It's **spring**. Look! The bears are awake. They are hungry!

3 Read and write the season.

1 The bears are eating. ______________

2 The bears are hungry. ______________

3 The bears are playing. ______________

4 The bears are sleeping. ______________

4 Do the Year in the Wild worksheet.

6 Lesson 5

1 Listen and number. 2.11

2 Listen again and draw the times.

Everyday English!

at the swimming pool | watching TV | at the playground | playing computer games

3 Listen and repeat. 2.12

4 Act it out.

What are you up to?

I'm at the club.

5 Make a Day in the Wild poster. Talk about your poster.

What time is it?
It's six o'clock. Look at the foxes. They're listening.

1 Read and listen. 2.13 What are the rabbits doing in the tunnel?

Lily's Wildlife Watch

The Wildlife Club is helping animals!

There's a new tunnel under the road. The animals can walk to the river. It's safe now. Let's see what the animals are doing.

It's six o'clock in the morning. Look! Rabbits! They're eating grass.

It's quarter to ten. The rabbits are listening!

It's two thirty. Where are the rabbits? Shhh! They're sleeping.

It's quarter past four. Look! The rabbits are walking in the tunnel. They're safe!

Our Values Lily says: "Help wildlife!"

2 Look at the clocks and write sentences about the rabbits.

1  It's two thirty. They're sleeping.

2  It's ______________. They're ______________.

3  ______________________________

4  ______________________________

3 How can you help wildlife? Go to the Values chart on page 119.

6 Review

1 Complete the puzzle.

listen watch eat read
walk sleep build

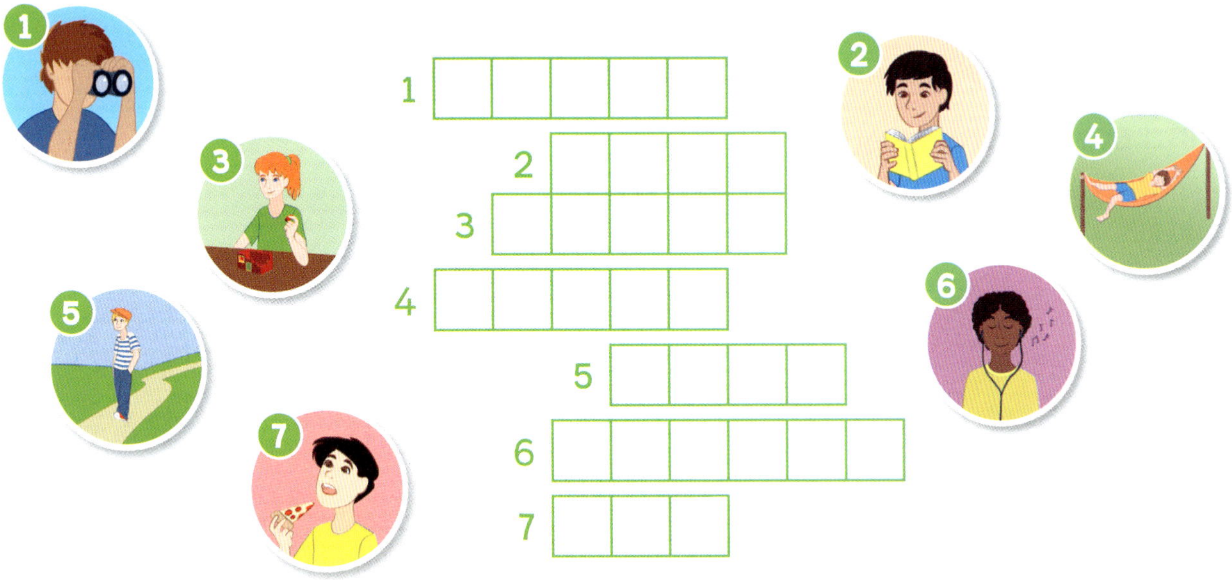

2 Follow. Read and correct the sentences.

1 It's twelve o'clock. They're building. They aren't building. They're eating.

2 It's four thirty. They're reading. They aren't ________. ________

3 It's quarter past five. They're drinking. ________

4 It's quarter to ten. They're watching. ________

Culture 3 Shopping : New York style!

1 Look at the pictures. What is the text about?

2 Listen and read. 2.14

3 Read and correct the sentences.

4 Project! Make a shopping street together.

A|X

shopping

There are lots of different places for **shopping** in New York City. A famous street for shopping is 7th Avenue. This is also called *Fashion Avenue* and you can see all kinds of interesting **fashion** here.

fashion

THE WORLD'S LARGEST STORE
macy's
★macy's
sunglass hut
sunglass hut

parade

This is Macy's Department store on 34th Street. Macy's is a really big store. It's over 150 years old. This store is famous for a Thanksgiving **parade** every year. There are lots of people, music, and dancers at the parade.

SABRETT
HOT PRETZEL
lunch

What time is it? It's twelve thirty. It's time for **lunch**! New York hot dogs are famous! You can buy them on the street. They're delicious!

1 The people on 7th Avenue are **sleeping**. ________________

2 You can see lots of interesting **animals** in New York. ________________

3 Macy's store is very **young**. ________________

4 Lunch is at **two** thirty. ________________

5 You can buy **toys** on the street for lunch. ________________

I want to eat a hamburger! Look! They're eating hot dogs.
I want to go shopping! Look! They're wearing cool clothes!
TOY SHOP

Exchange!

Which city is famous for fashion and shopping in your country? Do you like shopping?

7 The Open Day

Lesson 1

1 Listen and repeat. 2.15

2 Listen and number. 2.16

music
English
Cc Dd Ee Ff Gg
Hh Ii Jj Kk Ll Mm Nn
Oo Pp Qq Rr Ss Tt Uu
Vv Ww Xx Yy Zz
geography
+ - x =
2x1=2
2x2=4
2x3=6
2x4=8
5=10
=12
=14
8=16
math
PE

art
history
science
Hi, Stella! Find out more about school subjects!

3 Write. Which is your favorite subject?

1 

2 

3 

4 

5 

6 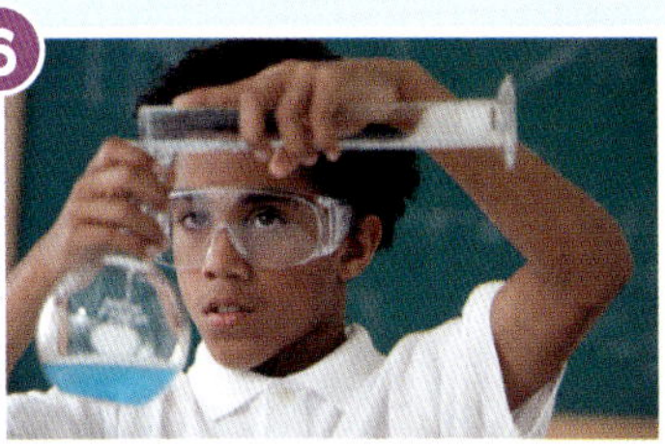

7 

8 

4 Ask and answer.

What's your favorite subject?
English!
Really? I prefer math.

School Mystery

1 Listen and read. 2.17 Who likes fruit? Act it out.

1
Look! This is the geography room.
Oh no! What's wrong?
Let's find out!
2
Look at this! Who is it?
I don't know, but he doesn't like science.
3
Listen! I think he likes PE!
Come on!
4
He isn't in here.
But look!
5
Hey! He likes art!
6
And it likes bananas! Look, it's a monkey!

How many subjects are in the story? Make a list.

Learn Grammar

He doesn't like science.
He likes art.

2 Listen and repeat. 2.18 Find sentences with ***likes*** in the story.

3 Look and say. Complete the sentences with ***likes*** or ***doesn't like***.

Joe likes geography.

He doesn't like art.

1 Joe ________________ art. He ________________ geography, science, and PE.

2 Stella ________________ PE and art. She ________________ geography or science.

3 The monkey ________________ geography, science or PE. It ________________ art.

HELP THE JUNIOR CREW! Find a ball in the story. Draw what's on it. Now go to page 120.

7 Lesson 3

1 Listen and repeat. 2.19 Which ones do you like? Make a ✓.

pottery ☐

drama ☐

gymnastics ☐

judo ☐

2 Read and write the names.

Stella Charlie Joe Lily

1 He likes gymnastics but he doesn't like judo. ________________

2 She likes pottery but she doesn't like drama. ________________

3 He likes judo but he doesn't like pottery. ________________

4 She likes drama but she doesn't like gymnastics. ________________

3 Look and write.

1 
____

2 
____

3 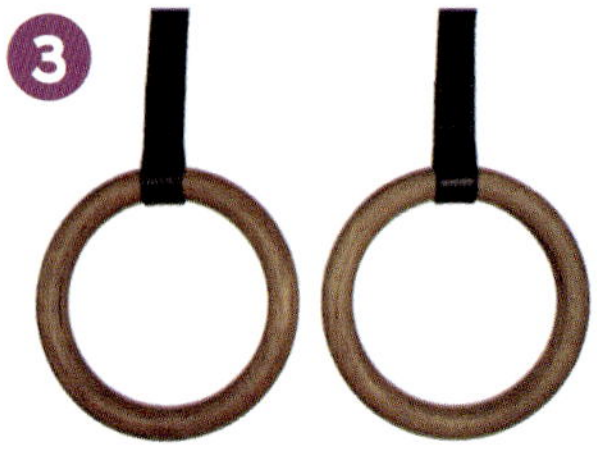
____

4 
____

Learn Grammar

Does he like gymnastics?
Yes, he does.
Does she like gymnastics?
No, she doesn't.

4 Listen and repeat. 2.20

5 Listen and match. 2.21 Ask and answer about Max and Kim.

1
2
3
4
A
B
C
D

6 Listen and sing. 2.22 Watch!

Song!

Does she like science? No, no, no.
She likes drama. Yes, yes, yes.
She likes drama and pottery, too.
Drama and pottery – yes, yes, yes!
Hobbies! Hobbies! These are her hobbies!
How about you? How about you? (Repeat)
Does he like music? No, no, no.
He likes judo. Yes, yes, yes.
He likes judo and gymnastics, too.
Judo and gymnastics – yes, yes, yes!
Hobbies! Hobbies! These are his hobbies!
How about you? How about you? (Repeat)

Grammar Does he like gymnastics? Yes, he does. No, he doesn't.

Practice Page 111

1 Look and find two school subjects in the text.

2 Read and listen. 2.23

Venn diagrams

Venn diagrams show **groups**. All the people or things in a group have something **in common**.

Look. We can make a **rule** about each group.

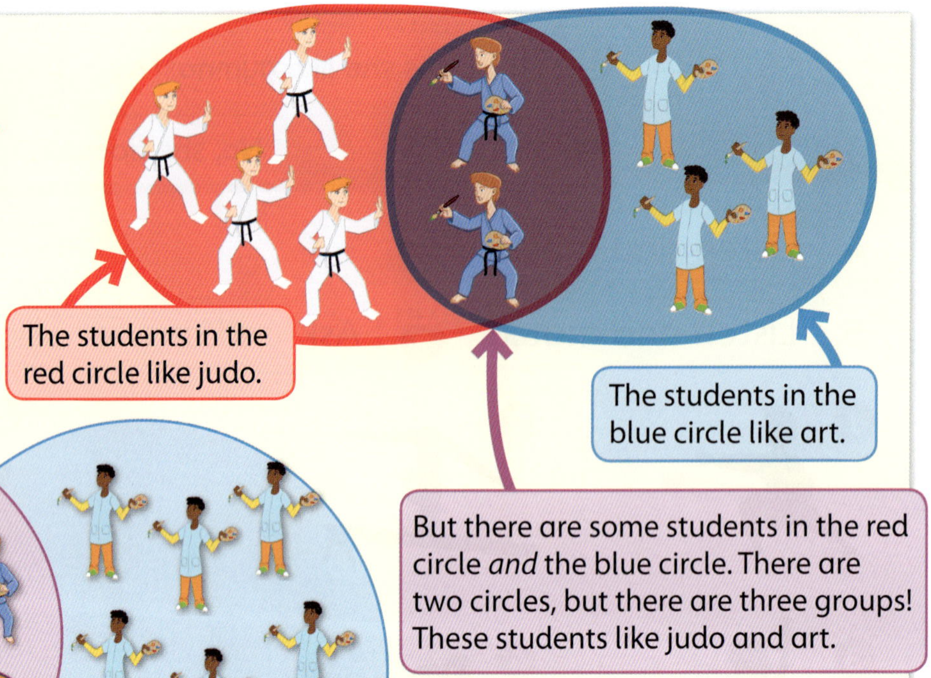
The students in the red circle like judo.
The students in the blue circle like art.
But there are some students in the red circle *and* the blue circle. There are two circles, but there are three groups! These students like judo and art.

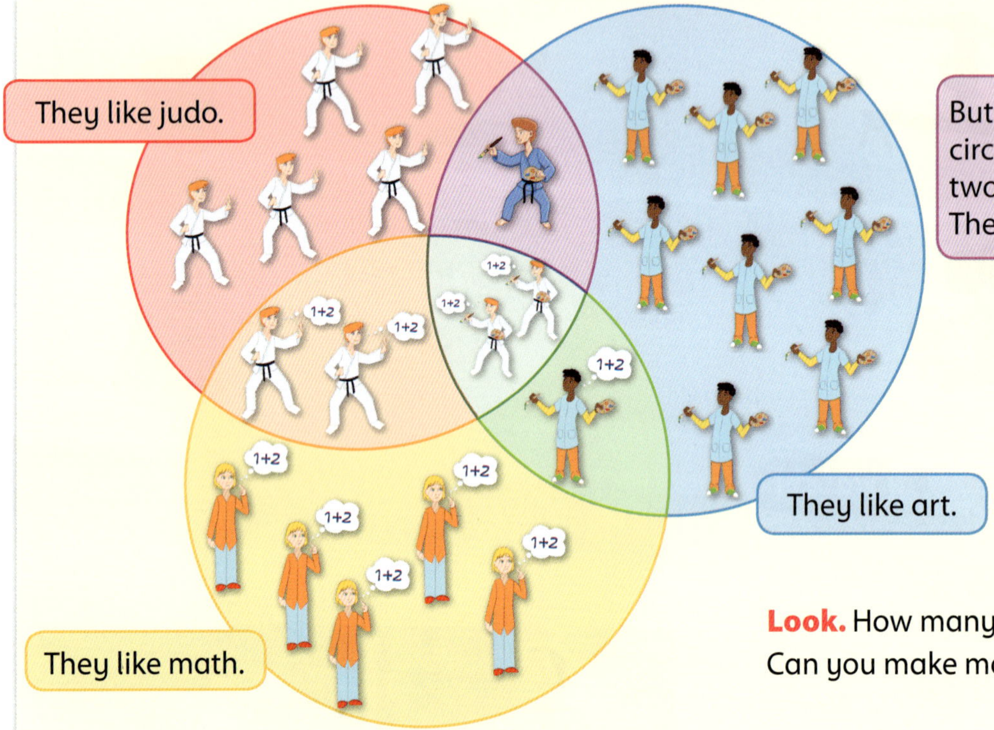
They like judo.
They like art.
They like math.

Look. How many circles? How many groups? Can you make more rules?

3 Look at the Venn diagram. Write how many.

1 How many students like math? ☐

2 How many students like math and judo? ☐

3 How many students like judo and art? ☐

4 How many students like math and art and judo? ☐

4 Do the Venn Diagram worksheet.

1 Listen. 2.24 What are Tom and Becky's favorite subjects?

2 Listen again and complete the faces with ☺ or ☹. Ask and answer about Tom and Becky.

Becky
Tom

Everyday English!

English judo geography pottery

I'm good at PE.

I'm not good at music.

3 Listen and repeat. 2.25

4 Act it out.

5 Make a list about you. Play *Last One Standing*!

This student is a girl.
She likes PE.

It's Ava!
Name: Ava
PE ☺
math ☺
history ☹
music ☹
English ☺☺☺

1 Read and listen. 2.26

Do Greg and Lisa have the same favorite subject?

Stella's Student Message Board

Hi, Stella! I'm Greg. My school is in London!

I like art and math.

My favorite subject is music. It's fun!

I don't like PE. I'm not good at it.

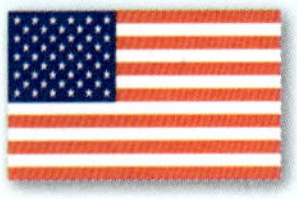

Hi, Stella! I'm Lisa. My school is in New York. You can see my classroom in the photo.

I like science and history.

My favorite subject is English! I'm really good at it. I don't like geography or art.

Our Values Stella says: "Try hard at school!"

2 Read again and answer about Greg and Lisa, using ***does*** and ***doesn't***.

1 Does Greg like music? Yes, he does.

2 Does he like PE? ______

3 Does he like art? ______

4 Does Lisa like geography? No, she doesn't.

5 Does she like English? ______

6 Does she like history? ______

3 Think about the subjects ***you*** can try hard in. Go to the Values chart on page 119.

 Writing practice Page 111

1 Complete the puzzle.

math history gymnastics art
geography pottery PE English

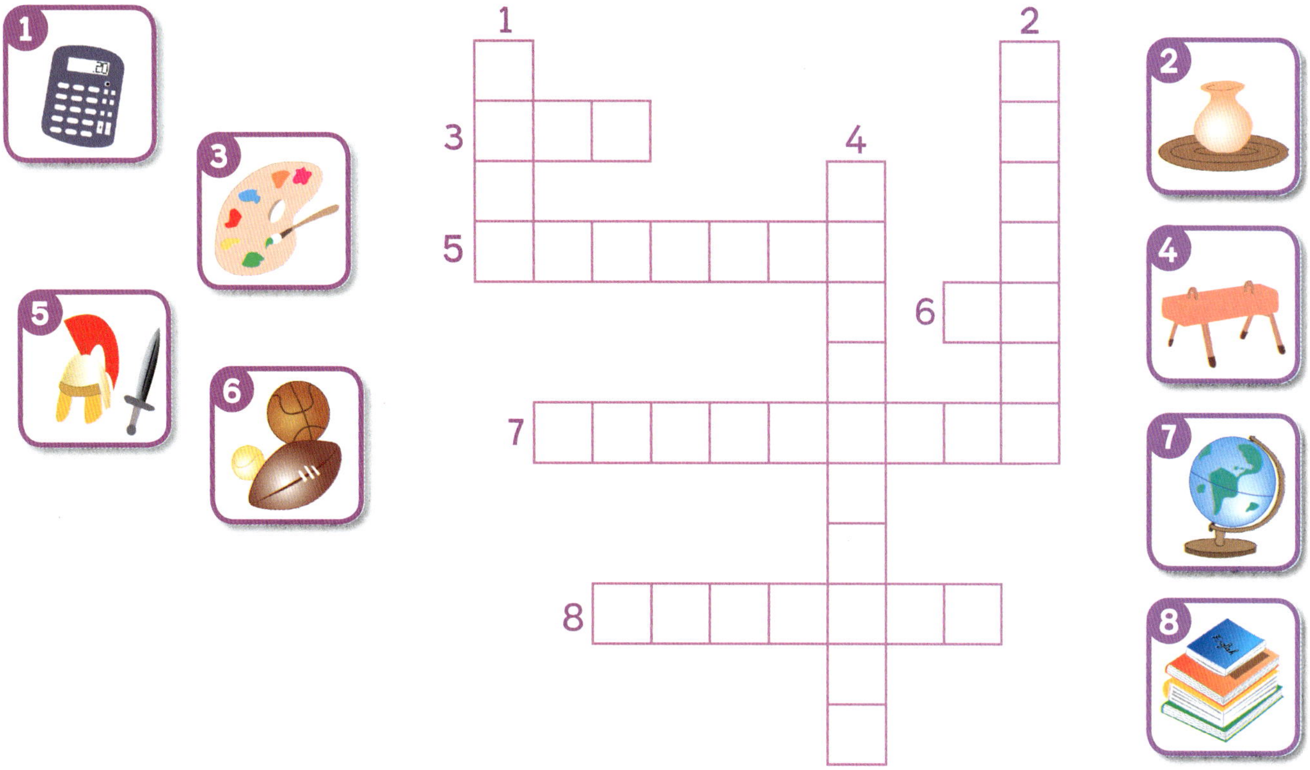
1
2
3
4
5
6
7
8

2 Follow. Answer the questions, using ***does*** and ***doesn't***.

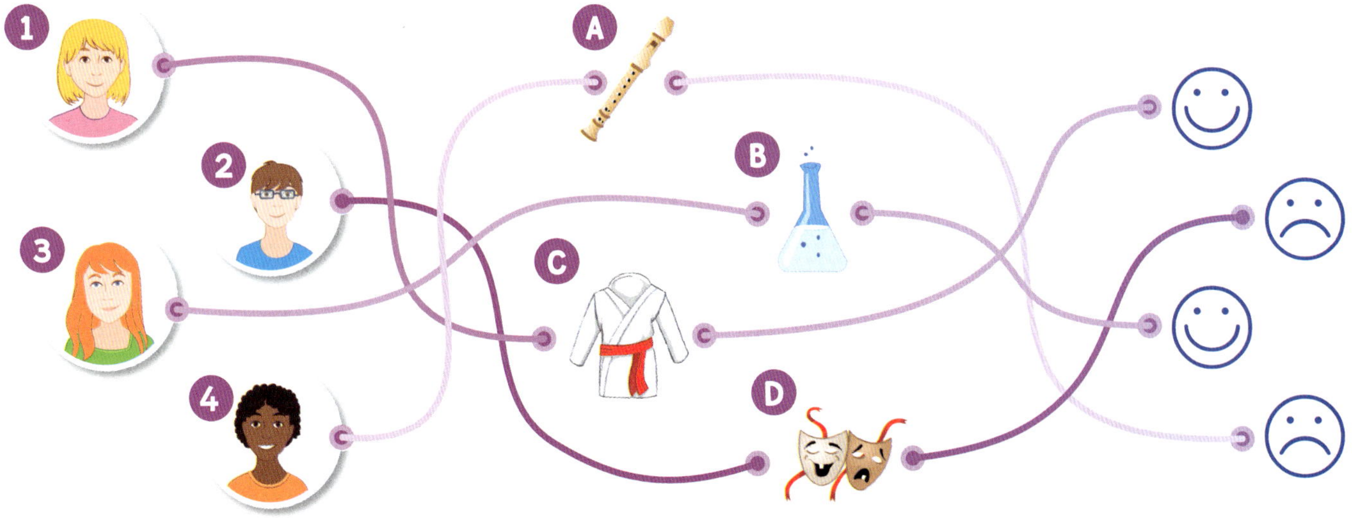
1
2
3
4
A
B
C
D

1 Does she like judo? Yes, she does.

2 Does he like drama? ______________

3 Does she like science? ______________

4 Does he like music? ______________

8 Are You Hungry?

Lesson 1

1 Listen and repeat. 2.27
2 Listen and number. 2.28

sausages ☐
potatoes ☐
tomatoes ☐
olives ☐
peppers ☐
mushrooms ☐

chili peppers
onions
Hi, Joe! Find out more about food and cooking!

3 Write. Which do you like on pizza? You can ✓ more than one!

1  ☐

____

2  ☐

____

3  ☐

____

4  ☐

____

5  ☐

____

6  ☐

____

7  ☐

____

8  ☐

____

4 Ask and answer.

What do you like on your pizza?
I like tomatoes and mushrooms. I don't like olives.

8 Lesson 2 The Cooking Contest

1 Listen and read. 2.29 What's on their pizza? Act it out.

1
A contest! Let's do it!
Great. I love pizza!
2
OK, we need tomatoes.
And we need cheese.
3
We need peppers.
And we need olives.
4
What are these?
Those are chili peppers. We don't need chili peppers.
Five, four, three, two, one, STOP!
5
Charlie, these aren't chili peppers!
THOSE are chili peppers!
6
We aren't the winners.
I need a glass of water!

How many foods are in the story?
How many more do you know?

Learn Grammar

We need peppers.
We don't need chili peppers.

2 Listen and repeat. 2.30 Underline these sentences in the story.

3 Look and number. Complete the sentences with ***need*** or ***don't need***.

1
- potatoes
- chili peppers
- tomatoes
- olives

2
- chili peppers
- olives
- sausages
- potatoes

3
- chili peppers
- tomatoes
- onions
- mushrooms

1 We __________ potatoes and tomatoes. We __________ mushrooms.

2 We __________ sausages and olives. We __________ tomatoes.

3 We __________ peppers. We __________ chili peppers and onions.

HELP THE JUNIOR CREW! Find a jacket. Draw what's on it. Now go to page 120.

8 Lesson 3

1 Listen and repeat. 2.31 What do you like in a sandwich? Make a ✓.

bread ☐

ham ☐

butter ☐

jelly ☐

2 Read and draw.

We don't need ham. We need butter and jelly.

We don't need jelly. We need bread and ham.

3 Complete the puzzle. Draw and write number 4!

1

2

3

4

5

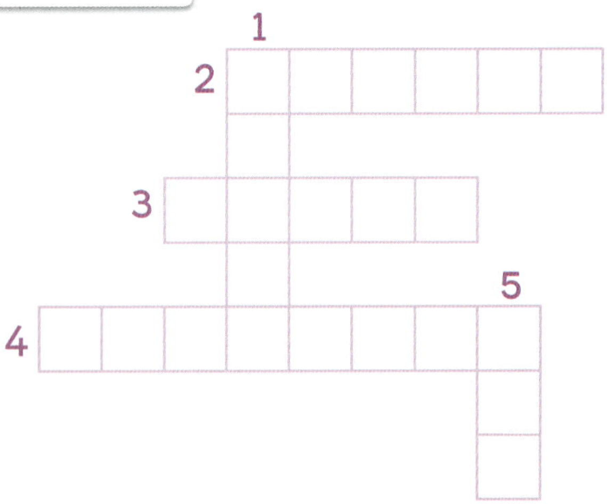
1
2
3
4
5

Learn Grammar

Do you need ham?
Yes, I do.
No, I don't.

4 Listen and repeat. 2.32

5 Listen and number. 2.33 Choose and write.

Yes, I do. No, I don't.

Do you need bread? ☐

____

Do you need butter? ☐

____

Do you need jelly? ☐

____

6 Listen and sing. 2.34 Watch! Song!

'A sandwich, a sandwich, a sausage sandwich!
A sandwich, a sandwich, a sausage sandwich!

I'm making a sandwich, a sausage sandwich.
I'm making a very yummy sausage sandwich.'
'Do you need bread?' 'Yes, I do.'
'Do you need butter?' 'Yes, I do.'
'Do you need sausages?' 'Yes, I do.
I'm making a very yummy sausage sandwich.'
'Do you need ham?' 'Do you need jelly?'
'No, I don't! It's a yummy sausage sandwich.'

'A sandwich, a sandwich, a sausage sandwich!
I'm making a sandwich, a sausage sandwich!' (Repeat)

Grammar Do you need ham? Yes, I do. No, I don't.

Practice Page 113

1 Look and say the foods that you know.

2 Read and listen. 2.35

Food Groups

To be healthy we need different foods from all these groups:

RICE
MILK
sun oil

We need these foods for **energy**, to run and walk.

We need these foods for **vitamins**, to stay well.

We need these foods for healthy **bones** and teeth.

We need these foods for strong muscles.

We need these foods to make the **building blocks** of the body!

We don't need these foods! They are **treats**!

Look. Which group is big? Which group is small?

3 Read and write.

We need ...

1 food like chicken, ham, and sausages for strong muscles.

2 food like potatoes, bread, and rice for ____________.

3 food and drinks like cheese and milk for ____________.

4 food like bananas, apples, tomatoes, and peppers to ____________.

4 Do the Healthy Meal worksheet.

8 Lesson 5

1 Listen. 2.36 Make a ✓ where they are.

2 Listen again. Follow and number.

- [ ] cafe
- [ ] kitchen
- [ ] supermarket
- [ ] market

butter

Everyday English!

butter bananas ham cheese

3 Listen and repeat. 2.37

4 Act it out.

We need tomatoes.

That's all, thanks!

Here you go. Anything else?

5 Write a Mega-sandwich Recipe for your friends. Ask, answer, and draw!

We need six sandwich fillings!
Six fillings! Do we need ham?
Yes, we do!
jelly
cheese
tomatoes
chicken
salad
ham

8 Lesson 6

1 Read and listen. 2.38 Which photo is Joe's special pizza?

Joe's Favorite Pizza

I love pizza! It's my favorite food. Let's make my favorite pizza! It's a special pizza!

We don't need tomatoes. And we don't need cheese. We don't need peppers or mushrooms or ham.

Here's my secret recipe!

We need jelly. And we need bananas. We need peaches and pineapple.

And we need chocolate! Chocolate and bananas are fantastic!

Look! It's a special treat.
It's a sweet pizza!

Our Values Joe says: "Remember to eat food from all the groups."

2 Read again and write Joe's answers, using ***do*** or ***don't***.

1 Do you need fruit? Yes, I do.

2 Do you need tomatoes? ____________

3 Do you need chocolate? ____________

4 Do you need cheese? ____________

5 Do you need ham? ____________

3 When can you think about the food groups? Go to the Values chart on page 119.

Writing practice Page 113

8 Review

1 Find eight foods. Write.

1 

____

2 

____

3 

____

4 

____

5 

____

6 

____

7 

____

8 

____

h	n	m	c	o	n	i	o	n	s
m	u	s	h	r	o	o	m	s	a
c	x	z	i	a	s	l	d	f	u
h	j	e	l	l	y	i	j	y	s
h	a	m	l	w	q	v	p	l	a
m	m	j	i	u	h	e	b	v	g
p	e	p	p	e	r	s	j	a	e
b	r	u	s	b	r	e	a	d	s

2 Look and complete the questions and answers. Use ***Do you need***.

butter

✗ 1 _______________ potatoes? No, I don't.

✓ 2 _______________ butter? _______________

✗ 3 _______________ peppers? _______________

✓ 4 _______________ bread? _______________

3 Look and write.

1 We need _______________.
We don't need _______________.

2 _______________ onions.
_______________ sausages .

Culture 4

Summer Camp

1 Look at the pictures. What is the text about?

2 Listen and read. 2.39

3 Read again circle the things that Lana mentions.

4 Answer the questions.

5 Project! Make a poster for your perfect summer camp.

DECEMBER 2015

months

Summer Camp

by Lana

In the USA, summer vacation is long – three **months** long! I like vacation, and I love **summer camp**!

summer camp

At camp we can do lots of sports. My brother Josh likes judo, but I prefer drama and playing tennis.

We can learn new things, too. I like pottery and painting.

graham crackers
marshmallows

The food at camp is delicious! Here's my favorite camp snack. They're called **s'mores**. You need **graham crackers**, chocolate, and **marshmallows**. We cook them on the campfire!

My favorite thing about camp is new friends!

1 Does Lana like summer vacation? ____________

2 Does Josh like judo? ____________

3 Does Lana like pottery? ____________

4 What's Lana's favorite food at camp? ____________

This camp has lots of activities. Look!
s'mores
milkshakes
food
Come to Shine On Summer Camp!
sports
tennis
judo
activities
campfires
drama
computer zone
Max likes sports, but I like art. We can do lots of things!

Exchange!

Is summer vacation in your country long? Are there lots of camps to go to?

Holidays

Carnival

1 What can you see in the photos?
2 Listen and read. 2.40
3 Do the Carnival Quiz. Circle ***Yes*** or ***No***.
4 Listen and read the carnival poem. 2.41
5 Project! Make a carnival mask.

parade

It's Carnival time in Rio de Janeiro!

Listen! It's the **parade**. Can you hear the music? This is *samba* music. Lots of **samba bands** play at Carnival! There are lots of carnival **floats**, too. You can see all the floats in the big parade in the *Sambadrome*. Look! They are very big and very beautiful.

samba band

float

feathers

Can you see the dancers in their costumes? They are wearing masks and **feathers**.

Carnival is noisy and fun! You can join in and dance, too.

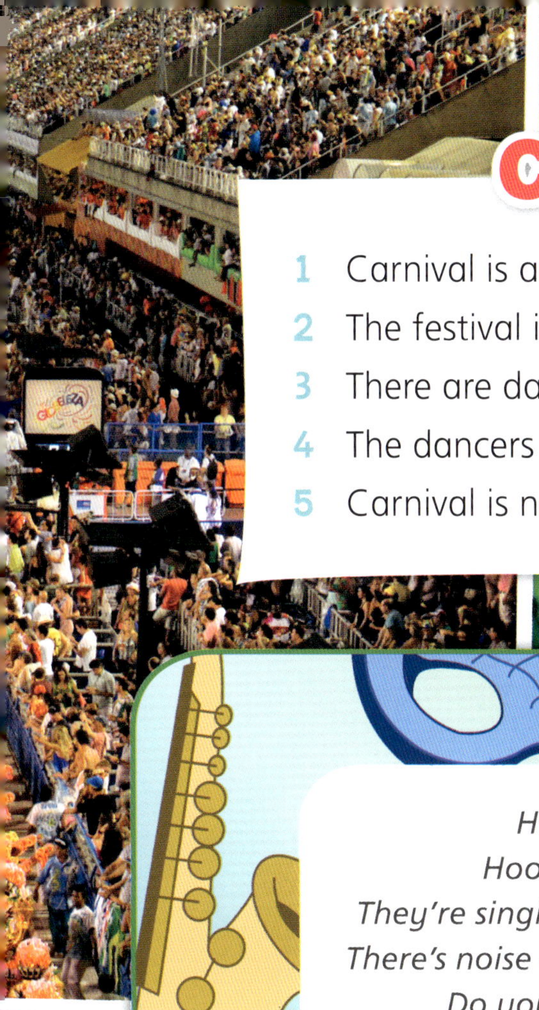

Carnival Quiz

1 Carnival is a festival in New York. Yes No
2 The festival is famous for samba music. Yes No
3 There are dancers and floats in the parade. Yes No
4 The dancers are wearing caps. Yes No
5 Carnival is noisy. Yes No

Hooray! Hooray! It's Carnival today!
Hooray! Hooray! Let's join in the parade!
They're singing in the market, they're singing in the street.
There's noise and music everywhere, and lots of food to eat!
Do you have a costume? Do you have a mask?
Let's go to Carnival! It's Carnival at last!

Look at Julio. He's wearing a mask with a blue feather and a purple feather. It's great.

Holidays

Christmas Eve

1 Who is the man in the photo?

2 Listen and read. 2.42

3 Circle seven Christmas words. Write.

4 Sing *Jingle Bells*. 2.43

5 Project! Make a Christmas Stocking!

stockings

It's Christmas Eve. It's the night before Christmas Day! The children aren't asleep. They're excited!

In the living room there's a Christmas tree. There are Christmas **stockings**.

Santa
reindeer

There's a snack and a drink for **Santa**. He's hungry on Christmas Eve! He has presents for all the children. He puts the presents under the tree and in the stockings for the next morning.

Listen! Can you hear **reindeer** on the roof? Shh! Santa is here!

To:
Santa

1  ______________________

2  ______________________

3  ______________________

4  ______________________

5  ______________________

6  ______________________

7  ______________________

s	a	n	t	a	s	t	m	a	s
t	r	e	e	r	i	p	o	f	t
a	j	i	k	e	l	p	p	s	o
k	e	s	g	i	f	r	d	t	c
l	r	t	z	n	s	e	v	q	k
s	t	a	r	d	a	s	m	d	i
s	r	g	t	e	n	e	n	p	n
v	e	s	x	e	t	n	a	l	g
d	e	c	o	r	a	t	i	o	n

Look it's Santa Claus, riding through the snow.
Look it's Santa Claus, riding through the snow.
Oh jingle bells, jingle bells, jingle all the way.
Santa Claus is riding, riding in a sleigh.
Oh jingle bells, jingle bells, jingle all the way,
Santa Claus is bringing gifts on Christmas day.

This is my Christmas stocking.

1 Practice Lesson 2

1 Look and write.

play baseball play tennis surf
skateboard play volleyball

1 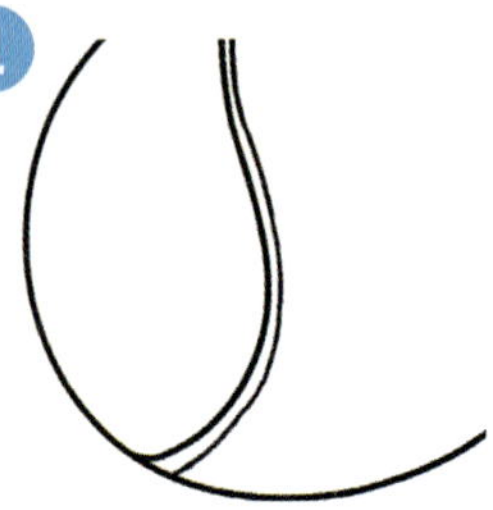

2 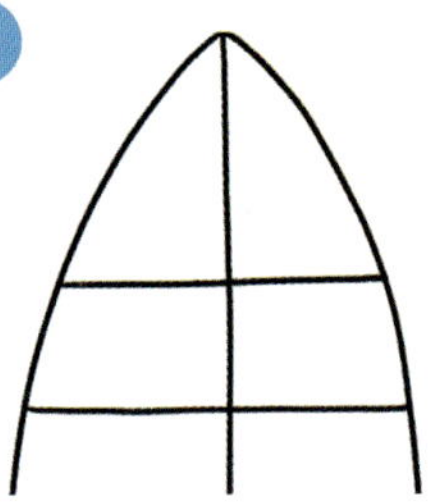

3 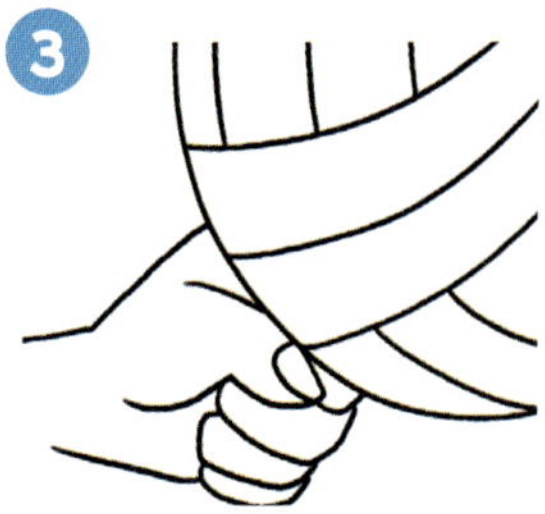

4 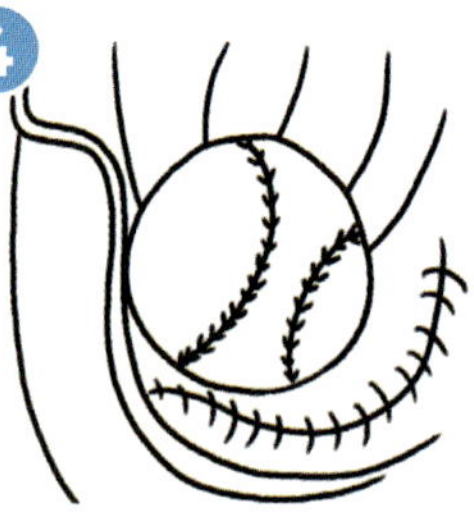

5 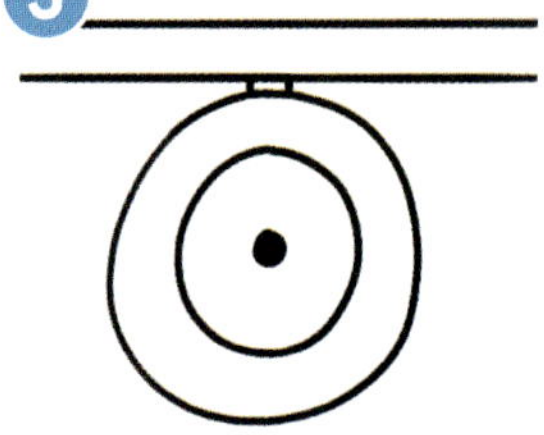

1 ____________ 2 ____________ 3 ____________ 4 ____________ 5 ____________

2 Look and write the answers using *can* or *can't*.

	 Leo	 Anna	 Luke
	✓	✗	✓
	✓	✓	✓
	✗	✗	✗

1 Can Leo ride a bike?
Yes, he can.

2 Can Anna play baseball?
____

3 Can Luke play tennis?
____

4 Can Luke play baseball?
____

3 Look again. Write questions and circle *Yes* or *No*.

1  (play baseball) Can he play baseball? **Yes** **No**

2  (ride a bike) ____________ **Yes** **No**

3  (play tennis) ____________ **Yes** **No**

4  (play baseball) ____________ **Yes** **No**

1 Practice Lesson 3

Yes, I can. ~~can she play baseball~~
Can you make videos   Can she surf

1 Read and complete.

Amy Amelia can ride a bike. But _can she play baseball_? ______________?

Stella I don't know. Let's ask Amelia!

Amy Good idea, Stella!

Amy ______________________, Joe?

Joe ______________

Amy Great! Go and find her!

1 Practice Lesson 6

1 Complete the interview with Charlie.

An interview with Charlie BMX champion!

By ______________

A BMX champion! Well done, Charlie! You can ride a bike very well!

Thanks! Thanks a lot!

Let's talk about other sports.  Can you _play tennis_?

No, I can't.

 Can ______________________________?

Yes, _I can_.

 ______________________________?

Yes, __________.

2 Practice Lesson 2

1 Who has these things? Look and write.

secretary director builder artist cleaner

1 
2 
3 
4 
5 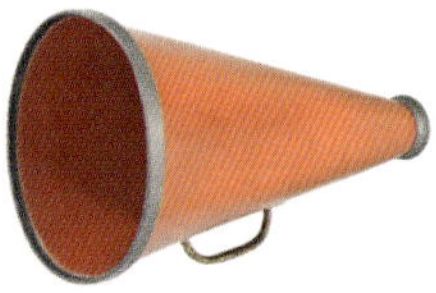

________ ________ ________ ________ ________

2 Look and number.

1 They're dancers.
2 They're reporters.
3 They're acrobats.
4 They're cleaners.

3 Complete using ***No, they aren't.*** and ***Yes, they are.***

1 Are they directors? No, they aren't. They're ________.

2 ________ acrobats? ________

3 ________ reporters? ________

2 Practice Lesson 3

1 Read and number the sentences in order.

[ ] Yes, I am. Look! It's finished!

[1] Are you an artist?

[ ] No, I'm not. I'm a builder.

[ ] Are you proud?

2 Practice Lesson 6

1 Write descriptions for Joe's blog.

(dancers) bored ✗

They're dancers. They aren't bored!

(artists) excited ✓ They're ________________.

____

(acrobats) afraid ✗ ________________

____

(directors) proud ✓ ________________

____

3 Practice Lesson 2

1 Find, count, and write.

turtles   fish   seahorses   seals

 ☐ ____________

 ☐ ____________

 ☐ ____________

 ☐ ____________

2 Look and write.

1  These are turtles.

2  This is a ____________.

3  ____________

4  ____________

3 Color and write a sentence.

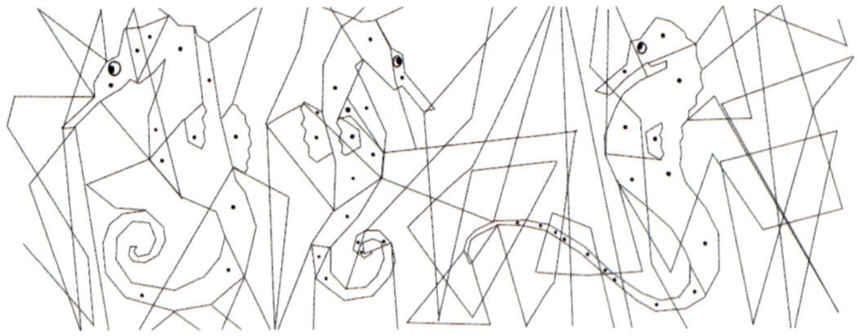

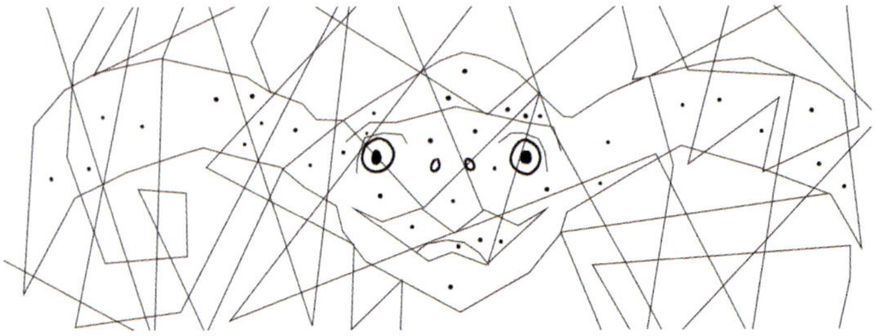

1 ____________

2 ____________

3 Practice Lesson 3

1 Read and complete.

's that? Those are are those? That's a

What are those?
__Those are__ seals.

What ________?
________ whale.

What ________
________ sharks.

3 Practice Lesson 6

1 Write a puzzle using words from the boxes. Show your friend.

shy smart funny friendly

deep water shallow water the beach

An eye A leg A tail A nose

These animals are ________.

________ animals like ________.

Here's some help! What's ________?

____

What are they? ________

1 What's missing? Write.

backpack umbrella money costume medal

1
2
3
4
5
724
1

1 ____________ 2 ____________ 3 ____________ 4 ____________ 5 ____________

2 Read and write *A*, *B*, or *C*.

A
B
C

1 Does he have a first aid kit? Yes, he does. Does he have an umbrella? No, he doesn't. ☐

2 Does he have a first aid kit? Yes, he does. Does he have a cap? No, he doesn't. ☐

3 Does she have a backpack? Yes, she does. Does she have an umbrella? No, she doesn't. ☐

3 Follow and write short answers.

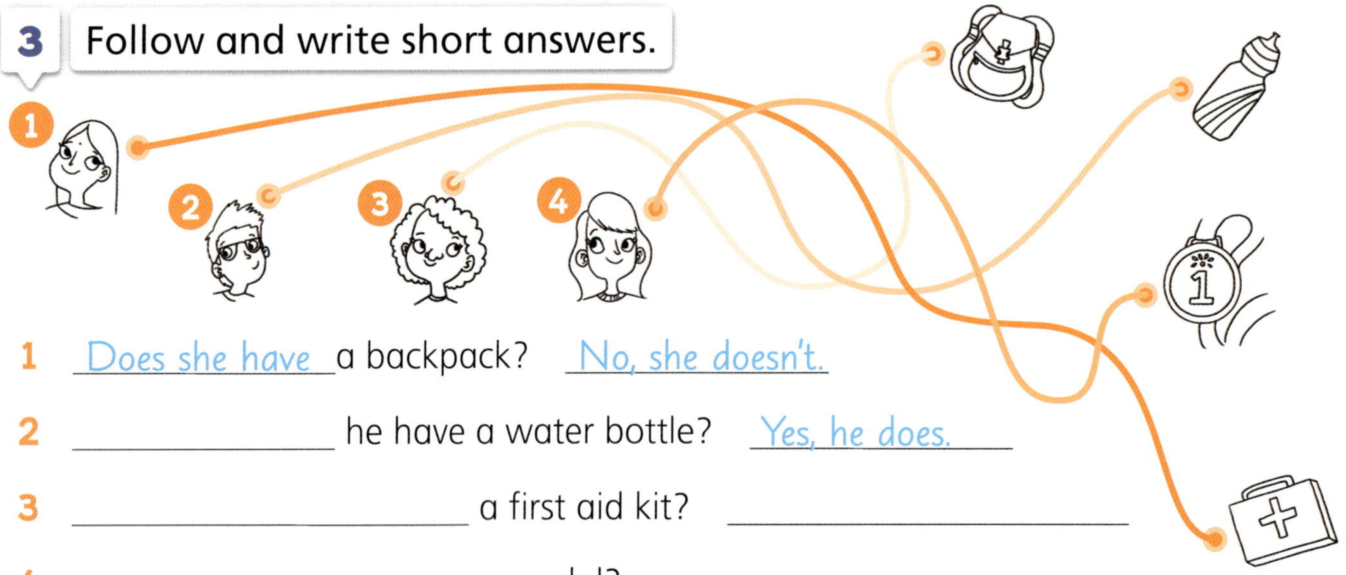
1
2
3
4
1

1 Does she have a backpack? No, she doesn't.

2 ____________ he have a water bottle? Yes, he does.

3 ____________ a first aid kit? ____________

4 ____________ a medal? ____________

4 Practice Lesson 3

I have | Yes, I do.
Do you have | No, I don't.

1 Read and complete.

FUN RUN

FUN

Charlie Do you have ______ any sisters?
Amy ______ I have one sister. Look! Here is my family!

Charlie ______ any cousins?
Amy ______ But I have two brothers. And ______ two aunts! Come on! Let's go to the picnic!

4 Practice Lesson 6

1 Imagine your friend is in the fun run. Write notes.

2 Draw your friend. Write a description.

FUN RUN checklist

Costume ✓ ______

Three useful things: ______

______

______

A fun runner!

By ______

Today my friend ______ is in the fun run!

(costume) He / She has a costume. Look! ______

(useful things ✓) ______

(useful things ✗) ______

And ______ has a  ______.

5 Practice | Lesson 2

1 Find, circle, and match.

1 

2 

3 

4 

hjleggingsserdresshjscarflgosneakerskgcoatajeanssandalsnsshirtlhdge

5 

6 

7 

8 

2 Circle the odd one out and write.

1 She isn't wearing a ___dress___.
She's wearing ___a shirt___.

2 He isn't wearing ______________.
He's ______________.

3 She ______________.
She's ______________.

4 ______________

____

5 Practice Lesson 3

1 Read and complete.

belt What's She's wearing
She's dress wearing

Stella Oh! What's my sister __________?
Mom ______________ wearing her new ______________. It's Grandma's party today.
Stella Today!

Dad Wow! ______________ Stella wearing?
Sister ________________ old jeans and a ______________!

5 Practice Lesson 6

1 Circle the clothes you like.

dress jeans sneakers sandals sunglasses gloves
scarf leggings belt watch shirt coat skirt sweater

2 Design an outfit for Stella's fashion page. Draw and write.

Fashion Page by ________________

______________'s wearing ________________.

____

____

____

____

Lesson 3 Page 55 Lesson 6 Page 58

1 What can you do with these things? Write.

walk build watch listen drink

1 

2 

3 

4 

5 

_______________ _______________ _______________ _______________ _______________

2 Look and write using the words in activity 1.

1  They're drinking.

2  _______________

3  _______________

4  _______________

5  _______________

3 Look and write. Read and make a ✓.

Φ	#	Δ	@		≈	Ω	Δ	†		Φ		∫	◊	Δ	Δ	‡	∞	†	*	
	h				a			n	'			s			e	p				.

Φ	#	Δ	@		Ω	Δ		◊	∞	∫	Φ	Δ	†	∞	†	*	
			y	'	r			l		s	t			i		g	!

1 

2 

3 

4 

6 Practice Lesson 3

1 Read and complete.

watching thirty o'clock
walking quarter past eating

It's two ______________.
They're ______________.

It's four ______________ .
They're ______________
the animals.

It's ______________ seven.
They're ______________
candy.

6 Practice Lesson 6

1 Look and write about three more photos from Lily's Wildlife Watch.

quarter to quarter past o'clock

sleep ~~build~~ listen

It's ______________.
There are birds.
They're building ______________.

____
There are otters.
____

____
There are foxes.
____

1 Look and write.

science geography PE art music

1 
______

2 
______

3 
______

4 
______

5 
______

2 Look and write.

	math	history	art	English
 Yoko	☺	☹	☹	☺
 Ali	☹	☹	☺	☺

Name: Yoko

She likes ______

and ______.

She doesn't like ______ or

______.

Name: Ali

He likes ______

and ______.

He doesn't like

______ or

______.

3 Complete the table with two ☺ and two ☹. Write about Anna.

 Anna				

Hello.

Name: Anna

Anna ______

and ______.

She ______ or

______.

7 Practice Lesson 3

1 Write the words in order to complete the dialogue.

Stella I have a message from Marco in Brazil.

Charlie like he Does judo?

____

Stella Yes, he does.

Stella And this is Jenny in the USA.

Charlie she Does pottery? like

____

Stella Yes, she does.

7 Practice Lesson 6

1 Make notes in the table about a friend.

My friend: ____________

☺ he/she likes	____________ ____________
☺ ☺ ☺ his /her favorite	________________________
☹ he/she doesn't like	____________ ____________

2 Draw and write an email about your friend to Stella's message board.

Stella's Student Message Board

Hi Stella! I'm ________________. This is my friend ________________.

☺ ______________________________________

☺☺☺ ___________________________________

☹ ______________________________________

1 Look and write.

chili peppers peppers mushrooms onions sausages tomatoes

Shopping List

 ____________

 ____________

 ____________

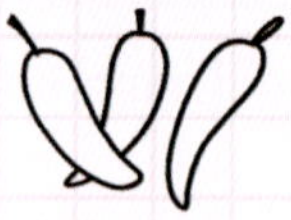 ____________

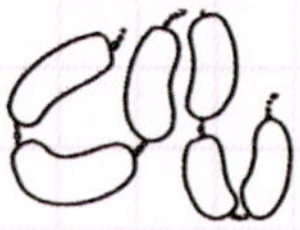 ____________

 ____________

2 Look at activity 1. Read and circle *Yes* or *No*.

1 We need tomatoes. **Yes** **No**

2 We need potatoes. **Yes** **No**

3 We need mushrooms. **Yes** **No**

4 We need olives. **Yes** **No**

5 We need sausages. **Yes** **No**

6 We need peppers. **Yes** **No**

3 Write about and draw your pizza toppings.

need don't need

1 We ____________ tomatoes.

2 We ____________ mushrooms.

3 We ____________ sausages and olives.

4 We ____________ peppers or onions.

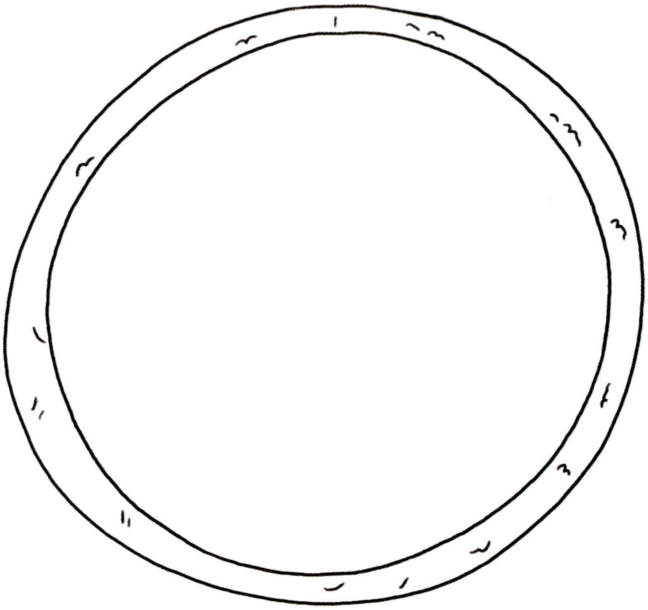

8 Practice Lesson 3

1 Read and complete.

No, I don't. Do you need
Do you need No, I don't.

Charlie ______________________ bread and butter?

Joe ______________________ My recipe is for pizza.

Charlie OK. ______________ ham, mushrooms, or olives? Oh look!

Joe ______________ Don't worry! I have an idea.

8 Practice Lesson 6

1 Read and circle the sweet pizza toppings.

peaches cheese tomatoes bananas mushrooms ham jelly
peppers candy olives chili peppers sausages pineapples

2 Check ✓ three toppings that you need, and ✗ three that you don't need. Draw and write a recipe.

My Special Pizza

____

____

____

____

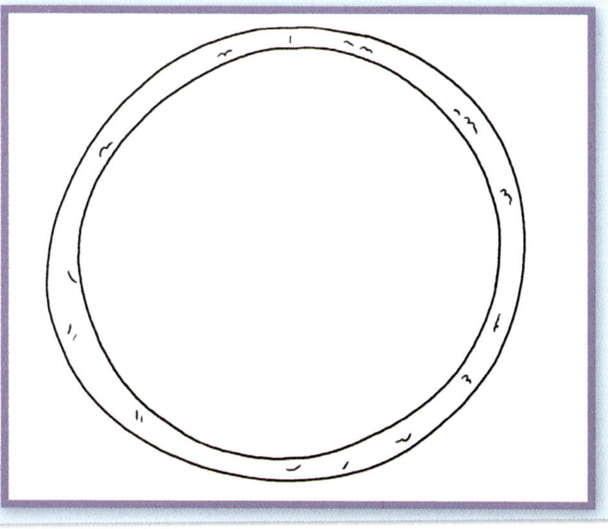

Grammar Reference

Question words

Question	Answer
What is it**?**	It's a message!
What time is it**?**	It's 3 o'clock.
Who is it**?**	It's Amy!
Where is it**?**	It's in town.
How many apples**?**	Three.
How old are you**?**	Eleven.

Possessive adjectives

Subject pronouns	Possessive adjectives
I	my
he	his
she	her

Can

Affirmative form	Negative form
I **can**	I **can't**
you **can**	you **can't**
he / she / it **can**	he / she / it **can't**

Interrogative form	Short answer	
Can you …?	Yes, I **can**.	No, I **can't**.
Can he / she / it …?	Yes, he / she / it **can**.	No, he / she / it **can't**.

Be

Affirmative form	Negative form
I **'m**	I **'m not**
you **'re**	you **aren't**
he / she / it **'s**	he / she / it **isn't**
they **'re**	they **aren't**

Interrogative form	Short answer	
Are you …?	Yes, I **am**.	No, I **'m not**.
Is he / she / it …?	Yes, he / she / it **is**.	No, he / she / it **isn't**.
Are they …?	Yes, they **are**.	No, they **aren't**.

Demonstratives

	Singular	Plural
Near	**This** seal	**These** seals
Far	**That** whale	**Those** whales

Have

Affirmative form	Negative form
I **have**	I **don't have**
you **have**	you **don't have**
he she **has** it	he she **doesn't have** it

Interrogative form	Short answers	
Do you **have** …?	Yes, I **do**.	No, I **don't**.
he **Does** she **have** …? it	Yes, he Yes, she **does**. Yes, it	No, he No, she **doesn't**. No, it

Present continuous

Affirmative form	Negative form
he she **'s wearing** it	he she **isn't wearing** it
they **'re wearing**	they **aren't wearing**

Present simple

Affirmative form	Negative form
I **like**	I **don't like**
you **like**	you **don't like**
he she **likes** it	he she **doesn't like** it
we **like**	we **don't like**

Interrogative form	Short answer	
Do you **like** …?	Yes, I **do**.	No, I **don't**.
he **Does** she **like** …? it	Yes, he Yes, she **does**. Yes, it	No, he No, she **doesn't**. No, it
Do we **like** …?	Yes, we **do**.	No, we **don't**.

Wordlist

Aa
acrobat
afraid
angry
art
artist
aunt

Bb
backpack
beach
beat
belt
bones
bored
bread
build
builder
building blocks
butter

Cc
cap
cartoon face
chili peppers
circle
cleaner
clothes
coat
costume
cousins

Dd
dancer
deep
design
director
dolphin
drama
draw pictures
dress
drink

Ee
eat
energy
English
excited

Ff
fall
fashion
feathers
first aid kit
fish
float
football
Friday
friendly
friends
funny

Gg
geography
gloves
graham crackers
groups
gymnastics

Hh
habitat
heart rate
history
hockey

Ii
in common

Jj
jeans
jelly
jog
judo

Ll
leggings
lines
listen
lunch

Mm
made of
make videos
marshmallows
math
medal
minute
Monday
money
monster
months
muscles
mushrooms
music

Oo
ocean floor
o'clock
octopus
olives
onions

Pp
parade
PE
peppers
play baseball
play basketball
play football
play soccer
play tennis
play volleyball
player
postcard
potatoes
potato chips
pottery
proud
pulse

Qq
quarter past
quarter to

Rr
rainforest
read
recycle
reindeer
reporter
ride a bike

rock pools
rule

Ss

samba bands
sandals
Santa
Saturday
sausages
scarf
science
seahorse
seal
seasons
second
secretary
shallow
shark
shirt
shopping
shy
skateboard
sleep
smart
s'mores
sneakers
souvenir
spring
stocking
stretch
summer
summer camp
Sunday
sunglasses
surf
surprised

Tt

take a break
take photos
team
thirty
Thursday
tomatoes
trash can
treats
Tuesday
turtle

Uu

umbrella
uncle

Vv

Venn diagram
vitamins

Ww

walk
warm up
watch (verb)
watch (noun)
water bottle
Wednesday
whale
winter
write stories

Our Values

Value question	Your notes:	My score
1 What sport can you try?		☆☆☆☆☆
2 When can you be part of a team?		☆☆☆☆☆
3 How can you take care of the ocean?		☆☆☆☆☆
4 How can you help your family and friends?		☆☆☆☆☆
5 How are you and your friends the same and different?		☆☆☆☆☆
6 How can you help wildlife?		☆☆☆☆☆
7 Think about the subjects you can try hard in.		☆☆☆☆☆
8 When can you think about the food groups?		☆☆☆☆☆

HELP THE JUNIOR CREW!

1 Look for the symbol from the story. Then find the place where the two symbols meet!

○	When	stop	you	Well done!	a	Club!	but	Best
◎	Who	start	he	Be careful!	an	Crew!	and	Cool
✱	Now	go	she	Don't worry!	it	Class.	can't	Happy
✗	How	visit	it	Hello.	at	Team.	can	Fun
△	What	like	they	Congratulations!	on	Show.	up	School
◆	Where	see	I	What's wrong?	in	Race.	down	Junior
■	Then	jump	we	Wow!	the	Game!	out	Town
➔	So	join	your	Let's go!	my	Day!	in	News
	✱	➔	○	△	■	◎	✗	◆

2 Write the word from activity 1.

Unit 6	Unit 3	Unit 4	Unit 1
______	______	______	______

Unit 8	Unit 5	Unit 7	Unit 2
______	______	______	______